# *Alone With God*

# ALONE WITH GOD

## By RICHARD WURMBRAND

LIVING SACRIFICE BOOK COMPANY
BARTLESVILLE OK 74005

Alone With God
©1988 by The Voice of the Martyrs, Inc.
First printing 1988. Second printing 1993.

Published by Living Sacrifice Book Company, P O Box 2273,
Bartlesville OK 74005-2273.

**Library of Congress Cataloging-in-Publication Data**
Wurmbrand, Richard.
    Alone with God / Richard Wurmbrand.
        p.      cm.
    Originally published: London : Hodder and Stoughton, ©1988.
    ISBN 0-340-42357-9
    1. Persecution–Romania–Sermons.   2. Jewish Christians–
    Persecutions–Sermons.   3. Political prisoners–Romania–
    Religious life–Sermons.   4. Sermons, English..   I. Title.
BR1608.R8W783   1993
272'.9'092–dc20                                          93-31634
                                                             CIP

# CONTENTS

# PROLOGUE

This is a book arising from a completely idle life, a life in solitary confinement in a Communist jail in Bucharest. I spent three of my fourteen years of prison alone in a cell, thirty feet below ground, with fifty pounds of chains on my feet and manacles on my hands, without ever seeing the sun, moon, stars, rain, or flowers, without paper or pencil, book or newspaper, let alone the Bible.

I never heard the slightest noise. The guards wore felt-soled shoes, and one could not hear their approach.

I never saw a human face except for the torturers, whose visage was something less than human.

I never saw a colour. I forgot that colours exist – violet, blue, red, yellow. Always I saw only the grey walls and my dull grey uniform.

Today thousands of Christians, Jews and other innocents are in a similar situation in Vietnamese, Chinese, Soviet, Mozambique, Ugandan prisons. They have long since ceased to ask themselves the usual questions that are in the minds of men. Instead, they ask, Do I live or vegetate? Is what I experience still existence? Is the whole of life only a nightmare? Does a God exist? Does existence exist? If God exists, so what? What is the good of His existing if He does not help us? If He cannot overthrow evil, how could He make a world?

During my years of solitary confinement I composed 350 sermons. I created them in my mind, because I could not write them down. I delivered them every night to an unseen audience. I also committed them to memory by using the simple mnemonic device of summarising them in short rhymes, which I repeated again and again.

When I was released from prison I did not sleep until I had committed all of them to paper. I managed to do so for 348 out of the 350.

As one puts a bouillon cube in boiling water to make soup, so I have diluted these very concentrated rhymes and reconstructed more or less my sermons.

It has not been difficult for me to reposition myself again in the atmosphere of that solitary cell, because even while free I continue to live in prison. I read only about the suffering Church. I write and preach about her, I work for her, I dream about her. Though the Jews left Egypt, Egypt did not leave the Jews. Whoever has passed through long years of imprisonment remains a prisoner even after he has been freed.

Some of the sermons I preached to my invisible congregation have already been published in two volumes, *Sermons in Solitary Confinement* and *If Prison Walls Could Speak*, which have been well received. Many readers have said they were edified. This is what encourages me to present a few more sermons delivered under those exceptional circumstances.

These sermons focus on the fundamental questions that torment every man in his subconscious. When one is faced with them under special circumstances as I have been, one realises that all other so-called "practical" thoughts about material or spiritual life are more often an escape from these ultimate concerns that plague the soul.

Thoreau says, "The art of life, of a poet's life, is, having nothing to do, to do something." Many great works of poetry have come out of a life of idleness, about which others have wondered. My idleness in the solitary cell has helped me to formulate questions. No answers are needed.

A man went to his pastor asking advice about some difficult problems. The pastor replied, "Kneel in church for two hours and you will have the answer."

The man said, "Do you really believe that the good Lord will appear to me in two hours' time and clarify my thinking?"

"No," said the pastor, "but you will realise in that time that you can live well enough with the questions unanswered and keep perfect trust in life."

This is the conclusion I have reached, too.

Jesus asked on the cross, "My God, my God, why hast thou forsaken me?" No angel came with a reply, but He was enabled to bear heroically the pain of the mystery together with the physical pain and end His earthly life with the triumphant shout, "Father, into thy hands I commend my spirit."

I hope my book will serve you to this end.

# HOW WE PASS THE TIME

DEAR BRETHREN AND SISTERS

I am sure you would like to know how we spend our time in prison. I must say, it passes quickly.

When I thought about the possibility of going to prison and heard stories of food deprivation and starvation, I was fearful. Now I realise that hunger is easy to bear. Sometimes a well-intentioned rich man thinks about the hunger of the poor more than the poor man thinks about it. Man has often dwelt in situations where food resources were scarce. Hunger has been the rule, satiety the exception. So man has elaborated mechanisms of adaptation to hunger. A Huguenot once survived forty-six years in prison. She probably did not have much to eat during that period, yet she survived.

I am not preoccupied with hunger.

For one thing, I travel a lot. Sometimes I hover for hours over Africa. I can see its darkness, its dense, dimly lighted jungles inhabited by wicked demons. I see Israel, the Arab countries, India, China, the vast ant-hill of Asia, a place of many crimes and few altars. I fly over Australia, Polynesia, the New Hebrides.

I remember reading how Patton brought the New Hebrides to Christ. Has his work remained? For years he preached in vain. Then he dug a well. When the natives asked him what he was doing and he explained, they laughed him to scorn. "Water comes only from above. It cannot come from below," they assured him. But it came. And when they saw it, they accepted Christ and all the teachings of the Church, though there exists not the slightest connection between the drawing of water from a well and the cleansing of sins through the blood of Christ.

Have Communists come in the meantime and shown them some greater "miracle", perhaps a tractor, which might convince them that the whole philosophy of Marx is true? Such are the foundations of vast systems of thought accepted by men. A boy enamoured of a Catholic girl will accept the dogma of the Pope's infallibility, of the bodily assumption of Mary, and of transubstantiation. He may believe in it sincerely. He might even be ready to suffer for it later. But the point of departure of his convictions is valueless.

I pass to America, the hope of the world for liberty, a hope which will deceive. I can see Scandinavia, England, Russia, France, Europe, the place of constant senseless wars in which nobody is ready to make the gesture of extending the first hand of real friendship.

But I travel even further. I have this trivial globe, and mankind. There are other stars and other beings and other endeavours to stem the stream of evil.

From my stellar pulpit the whole world is my parish. I pray for all of it, though from a practical standpoint I can be only a rank-and-file soldier on a very small sector of the front.

Nobody can fight without interruption. I tap the Gospel by Morse code through the wall. But I must also have some relaxation. The discussions by code embrace many topics: religion, politics, and stories from private life. Sometimes a prisoner simply entertains by telling a joke.

Tonight I heard a good one:

Three men sat in a prison cell and asked each other why they had been arrested. One said, "I was arrested for sabotage."

"What did the sabotage consist of?"

"I came to my job five minutes late."

"And why are you in prison?"

"I am in for spying."

"And what did the spying consist of?"

"I came to the factory five minutes early, and they thought I was trying to spy on its secrets."

Then the third was asked, "Why are you in prison?"

"Because I came to work punctually, which meant that I must have connections in the West who sent me a good watch."

I pay my dues to human nature and laugh a little. But I weep a little about the tragic background of this joke, because the three persons mentioned really sit in prison. Under Communism all roads lead to jail.

But then I remember that I have better things to do than amuse myself or brood about such things. I can spend some hours in the communion of saints. People usually imagine them to be somewhere far away, although the Bible tells us that they encompass us (Heb. 12:1).

So I evoke the story of St. Gerard, a child who once went into the church to the statue of the holy virgin with the little Jesus and said to the Child: "I am so alone; I have no one to play with," whereupon Jesus descended from the statue and played with him. I recall the story of St. Bernard of Clairvaux, who also stood before a statue of Jesus and told Him how he loved Him and how he thirsted after the love of the Saviour. His biography says that Jesus again descended from the statue and hugged St. Bernard.

That other men do not have the same experience as

Gerard and Bernard of Clairvaux is their own fault! Every man can see outwardly only what he has within. He who harbours no God in his heart does not meet God, and he who denies the possibility of a saint having intimate contact with God neither plays with the child Jesus nor is hugged by Him. For a child, these stories reflect life, just like all other happenings. "Except ye become as little children..." said the Master.

I remember when my son Mihai first told me that he had seen Jesus walking through our rooms. He did not tell me this when it happened because it did not seem extraordinary to him. He told me a few months or perhaps a year later. The supernatural was the natural in our home.

I spend my hour among these beauties. Whoever does not deliberately choose them will pass his time in ugliness. Modern art expresses the ugliness of the human soul that has abandoned Christ and the saints.

It is said that a match-maker introduced a young man and a girl, who were intended to marry. The young man was indignant after seeing the girl and said: "How did you dare show her to me? She has only one eye, her nose is crooked, her lips are lop-sided. She is thick as a barrel but has a very thin neck. Her hands are much too short. I cannot marry such a girl!"

The match-maker replied, "Well, what should I do with you if you are a man who does not appreciate Picasso?"

Communism is to politics what Picasso is to art. As he distorts his models on canvas, the Communists contort the bodies of their adversaries.

A Communist officer told me, "If God created man, he created him to be tortured. This is obvious. There are some four or five zones of the human body whose touch produces pleasure. But there is not an inch of the human body which cannot ache. You can torture a man by pulling his hair or by beating him on the soles of his feet. Man is created for torture, and I merely fulfil the Creator's will."

When you ask them why they beat, they laugh and give their standard reply, that boys' tops cease to spin if they are not whipped. And man and a wooden toy are all the same to them! Another standard reply is that the more heads you cut off, the taller you appear yourself! And that is exactly what they did in Romania, cutting off the heads of not only their adversaries but even their comrades who were competitors.

You try to counter with an obvious argument: "You have two sets of doctrines which do not square with one another: on one side Communism, which means even etymologically 'to seek the good of the community,' and on the other hand this treading on human individuals and their rights." The police officers reply indifferently, "What if the doctrines do not square? We have methods to make them square. Everything squares under a whip."

They use this whip a great deal. They enjoy ugliness. I enjoy beauty.

And so between a whipping and a joke, a pleasant journey and immobilisation in heavy chains, between hunger and philosophising that it is easy to bear (if so, why do I have to convince myself about this easiness?), between the communion of saints and the mockeries of devils unleashed against us, the time passes quickly.

Don't worry about us. All things will pass. This too will pass. Amen.

# DESIRE TO ESCAPE FROM THE "I"

DEAR BRETHREN AND SISTERS

In at least one respect I am like St. Anthony the Great. He never washed himself. I did not take a bath in years either. He slept in a tomb in order to remind himself constantly that this is the abode in which all earthly life inevitably ends. My cell is also like a tomb. It is thirty feet beneath the earth. The few planks which constitute my bed could as well become my coffin. I don't fear death. I am in a tomb without having died.

What will be my future?

At this moment I am completely useless. My life consists of eating watery soups and getting endless beatings. The sticks are all alike. They make the same noise when they fall upon my back. The pain does not impress me much any more. Nothing ever happens in my life. Why should I wish to prolong my existence in this world? That I may be released? Of what use can a broken man be in freedom?

And if I recover? I will deliver some sermons again. Previously, when preaching on the subject of the blood of Christ, I had contemplated how to form the sentences more beautifully, instead of feeling the horror of Christ's suffering and living the love which prompted Him to endure it. In one of the first Christian sermons I ever heard, the pastor yawned while preaching about Calvary. How unlike Dickens who, while reporting for a

newspaper a speech in Parliament on the sufferings of
the poor in Ireland, was so overcome that he was unable
to take it down in shorthand.

A man speaks about the sufferings of a poor God and
yawns. No wonder the audience yawned too. Pastors
and flocks are fed up. They are also fed up with good
sermons. They are too wise. Fools for Christ are needed,
but I am not one of them. I don't see any point in being
free.

Neither do I wish to keep my "I" in eternity. Why
should I care for life after death when I have none before
death? My "I" has simply become uninteresting to me. I
am as little concerned about its eternal destiny as about
what will happen to it tomorrow. I wish to be an "I" no
longer. I reject my "I". My desire is to be a "he".
"When he shall appear, we shall be like him" (1 John
3:2).

I once brought to Christ a Jew who was over ninety
years old. He told me of a dream in which he saw himself
in heaven and asked, "Where is Wurmbrand's place?"
But he received no answer. The question was probably
still pending. At least, that was what I thought when he
told me his dream. Now I am inclined to think that there
will be no "Me" there. Why should I care about
receiving a crown, which I will cast at His feet anyway,
over-awed by His majesty when I see Him? (Rev. 4:10)
Is it not best to finish completely with the "I" and
become "He"?

There was a time when I was obsessed with erotic
fantasy. My head was a merry-go-round of lustful
images. At first I fought against them in vain. Then I
said to myself that if marriage is a symbol of the union
between Christ and His Church, erotic imagination and
love-play, which are basic to marriage, might also have
a holy sense. When I stopped worrying about these

fancies, they lost their importance.

Now my conscience has been almost freed from existence. It is independent of the "I" and lives the imaginary life of being "He".

Is this sheer madness, like so many other things happening to me, or am I one of the privileged few who have fulfilled the commandment of Christ to deny the "self"? But if I have denied the self, who is the one interested in knowing if this has really happened? Who then is happy that the denial of the "I" has occurred? We are running around in a vicious circle. One must have a very strong "I" and be a giant in faith to reject his "I", which is not only all that he has but also all that he is. Whoever burns the candle at both ends must have a great and glorious candle to burn. And what happens to the strong "I" who has rejected the "I"?

Jesus did not have the rich psychological vocabulary we have. He could not have spoken in Hebrew about the self, the ego, the id, the many complexes we worry about today.

I have always used Biblical language, speaking exactly as Scripture does about denying the self. In more precise modern language, I imagine that what Jesus meant us to leave was the ego.

In my dealings with people I have discovered that you don't impress them by showing how smart you are. You win them rather by sitting at their feet and giving them a chance to teach you. Even an idiot can teach something. The usual attendance in churches is composed of men of lower IQ than that of a pastor. If the pastor does not know stupidity but only intelligence, he will not be fruitful.

We have to learn from another to raise *his* ego. The ego is the desire to be superior. It is the high opinon one holds about oneself and one's achievements. I don't believe as does Freud that the strongest desire of a man is the sexual urge, though it is enormous. The strongest desire is to uphold his ego, to appear valuable before his fellowmen.

Respect another's ego, but renounce your own. I believe this is what was meant by Jesus' commandment to deny the self.

There is a tension in us because the ego is torn apart in the effort to present a more beautiful image before the world. Tension ceases when we become indifferent to what people think about us. I have been a pastor much beloved by my family and my congregation, and much hated by anti-Christian Jews because of my missionary work to win Jews for Christ. Now I am only despised and mocked by every man with whom I speak, because I speak only with wardens and interrogators. What do their opinons count? For Juliet it was enough to be loved by one single young man in Verona. Others might have passed near this girl of fourteen without even casting a glance at her. She was happy.

I don't know how much I have achieved, but I wish to lose not the self – I have come to the conclusion that such an endeavour is chasing after the impossible – but self-assertion. The Tao-Te-King says, "Clay is moulded into a vessel, but the ultimate use of the vessel depends upon the part where nothing exists. Doors and windows are cut out of the wall of a house, but the ultimate use of the house depends upon the parts where nothing exists." I wish to become such a useful nothing.

I am in the lowest social category, a man who will probably die in prison, sentenced for crime. But I am content to be so low. I have so little to renounce now. It seems ridiculous even to attempt to give up self-assertion. What have I to assert and before whom?

For a long time I have played with the ideas of what I

would do if I were a pope, a king, a polar explorer, again a little child. Then I became pious and thought about the eternal salvation of what I recognise to have been my ego. Now I fancy only to be "He". I don't strive to be He. I believe I am. Psychotherapists would call it the Messiah complex. Well, they would have applied the same diagnosis to Him, and they would not even have been mistaken. He really believed He was the Messiah. And I believe I belong to His body, as much as His brain and His heart belonged to His body during His earthly life. Every part of Him was He. And I am He. Luther wrote "The Christian is Christ." Only this He lives eternally. He does not need the appendix of a little "I".

When Michelangelo finished his *Pietà*, he exclaimed, "Only the marble separates me from my statue." I would say, "Only 120 pounds of flesh separate me from being fully He."

"To the only wise God our Saviour, be glory and majesty, dominion and power, both now and ever. Amen."

# TO KNOW THE HOLY THING

MY BELOVED

It is only natural that nobody knows about these sermons of mine. People live during the day on words. I speak silences during the night.

We have been put in subterranean cells, thirty feet below the surface, where no noise is heard. Our captors did not know that ascetics have always sought out solitude, silence, eventlessness, a life in which nothing disturbs the spirit, as ideal circumstances for their development.

For me it is all right to be in a cavern, locked away. Thoughts can pass through thick walls. And it is ideal to have a life without events. A man from a neighbouring cell asks, "What day is it?" I can give the answer, "Every day God is my date. I have no other."

Nor is silence a torture for me. Jews have been prepared for silence even through their language.

The Hebrew language has silent letters. The *Aleph*, first letter of the alphabet, is a scarcely audible breathing, and the *ayïn* a trifle stronger breathing but still almost inaudible.

The Lord said to John, "I am the Alpha and the Omega" (Rev. 21:6). This is how the words appear in the Greek New Testament. But Jesus and St. John were both Jews, so they probably spoke Hebrew. How would Jesus have said that he is the *Aleph*? Would he have pronounced the name of the letter, or would he have simply breathed on the apostle as He had done on another occasion, and would this breath have been the *aleph*? As for the *tav*, the last letter of the Hebrew alphabet, it was written at that time as a cross. Would Jesus have made the sign of the cross? When did this sign begin to be used as a holy sign? We find an abundance of crosses in the catacombs, perhaps as a result of this conversation.

There are different signs written below and above the Hebrew letters to make them pronounceable. They are what we would call vowels in other languages. But not all of these can be heard. The *shevah*, the first "vowel" of the Hebrew Bible, is in reality only a half-vowel. It is a very short "e". A half-vowel (*hataph-segol*) begins the name of God, *Elohim*. *Brit*, the Hebrew word for "covenant", also has a half-vowel at the beginning. It has to be pronounced quickly. It is as if the structure of the Hebrew language itself would teach one to speak little about holy things. One learns most about them in silence.

The name which we spell "Jehovah" starts in Hebrew with a very short vowel almost without forming the lips for it and finished with a silent "h". By the way, Jehovah, like all substantives and names ending with a "h", is a feminine name. Jeshuah, the name of Jesus in Hebrew, is also a feminine name. It is like calling a boy "Helen" or "June".

The earliest evidence of man's religion, outside the Biblical line, is the worship of the female. Archaeologists have dug up a whole galaxy of female figures from about 2500 BC, usually of naked women, standing or seated, often pregnant. The earliest temple compounds in the whole world, dating from around 3000 BC in Mesopotamia were dedicated to the worship of the Mother, some temples even being suggestively of oval form. The first recorded extra-Biblical divine being was a goddess. The word for Spirit in Hebrew, *ruah*, is a feminine substantive.

I had never thought about these things before imprisonment. Now they have become extremely important to me. Protestants have weighed exaggerated veneration of the virgin Mary against the teaching of the Scriptures. It is like judging the loud cries of tortured men with Bible verses teaching soft speech. This great veneration for and appeal to Mary must have originated with men who suffered terrible deprivations and at the same time passed through a dark night of the soul in which they could not apprehend the nearness of Jesus. In an extremity of torture, prisoners always cry, "Mother".

I have deviated completely from what I had intended to say. It is because for the first time I preach what I think. In the pulpit, pastors preach what they have thought of in their study while preparing their sermons. Congregations would wonder very much if one Sunday morning their pastors were to tell all the wandering thoughts that pass through their minds as they give their prepared message. They have doubts just when they preach certainties, attractions towards a sin just when they thunder against it. They surely would not thunder if it did not exercise such an attraction.

But you must bear with me. I come back now to my subject.

The surroundings of our solitary confinement are conducive to silence. The wardens have felt-soled shoes. We do not hear them walking up and down the corridor. They rarely speak to us. Everyone sits alone in his cell without any book or writing material and, according to his preparation, broods or meditates, loses himself in erotic imagination or makes practical plans for an uncertain future.

Rarely do we hear the cry of somebody being beaten because there are special rooms for beatings and torture somewhere else. Sometimes we hear the ravings of someone who has gone mad. But he would be quickly gagged or given some injection. And then again, silence.

The only real and more constant interruption of the silence is the "telephone", the tapping signals in Morse code through the walls or the pipes of the central heating. Usually the wardens do not disturb this. They know our codes and are interested in listening in on what we communicate to each other. There are always the naïve few who allow some secrets to slip through their communications.

The number one topic of all conversations is divining when and how the Americans will come. We set dates by which time we feel we surely will have been freed. With absolutely no possibility of obtaining real information, except perhaps on a bit of paper found in the toilet or from a prisoner arrested six months before, nevertheless we tap to each other estimates and commentaries on the most "recent" sensational events.

Frogs living in a well discuss the ocean they never saw. Insects living only a summer talk about skiing. Men existing in tiny subterranean cells with minds long since gone mad philosophise about the effects of world events on them, events of which they know nothing.

The conversations do not last long. The invasion of sound gives way to the deep silence in which I can meditate I do not desire to be free. I *am* free. The tyrant of Syracuse once went to the slave-philosopher Epictetus and told him, "I'll pay the ransom for you and you will be liberated."

Epictetus replied, "Why do you care about me? Free yourself."

"But I am a king," said the amazed tyrant.

"This I contest," was the answer of the philosopher. "He who masters his passions is a king even while in chains. He who is ruled by his passions is a slave even while sitting on a throne."

Real freedom does not depend upon external circumstances. There exists the wonderful liberty of which the children of God partake, even when in straitened circumstances or trammelled by prison walls.

I am not freed of passions but I am free from the desire to know trifles. What matters when I will be free? The period since my birth has been brief. In the millennia before I was born the world went on without considering my presence in it important. I am sure that events continue their course undisturbed by my absence.

Nor do I wish to know other things. I wish to know only "the holy thing" about which Luke speaks in mystery (Luke 1:35). One day of His, one day of being *with* Him, is worth a lifetime of knowledge *about* Him, which is putting into human words the inexpressible.

Why my Beloved keeps me in prison I do not know. But I remember from *A Midsummer Night's Dream*, which I consider the profoundest of Shakespeare's plays, these words: "The course of true love never did run smooth ... (To be crossed is) as due to love as thoughts and dreams and sighs, wishes and tears." There has never been a great love without its share of enigma and drama. So also is the love between Jesus and me. Let Him do as He likes. Reason will never fathom His ways. Generally "reason and love keep little company".

God did not free Daniel. He left him in the lions' den until he was freed by Darius, who threw him there. Perhaps I too will be freed by the Communists, not by the

Americans or the miraculous intervention of God. But I do not lose much time thinking about this.

I wish to know God in the supreme sense. The Hebrew word for "to know", *iada*, and the Greek *gnosis* are both used also for union between husband and wife. I wish to know him intimately, to have the beatific vision, to see "the holy thing" in its fullness.

Life and death depend upon this.

I once told a Jewish boy of twelve, "If Jesus is the Messiah and you reject Him, your soul will be eternally lost," to which he answered earnestly, "But it is also the other way around. If Jesus is not the Messiah and you adore Him, you are eternally lost." And so we sat down to find out which of us was right.

The life of Saul of Tarsus, the persecutor, centred around Jesus long before he met Him on the road to Damascus. He had ordered Christians to be killed. Whether Saul was a national hero fighting against a dangerous impostor or a killer of innocent believers in the true Saviour depended upon the reality of the vision he had before his eyes.

Mary Magdalene waited at the tomb of Jesus. He had forgiven her many sins. Everything depended on what would happen that Sunday morning. If He were resurrected, the remission of sins granted by Him was valid. If He remained entombed, her sins would return and she would have added to her former transgressions the grave offence of having followed a false Messiah.

I am in the same situation. If Jesus is not the Truth, I will have squandered my life and youth in useless suffering. If He is, I will have gained everything.

Will he come once to free me from my doubts?

No thief could sleep if he knew that a sack of gold lay in the next room. I also spend one sleepless night after another. But some day I will get hold of "the holy thing".

I surely prefer Communists to lukewarm, nominal Christians. If Jesus is not the Saviour, if He was a deceiver or one deceived or, as some say, a psychopath, things cannot be left as they are. It becomes the duty of every honest man to go from door to door to warn men of the pernicious influence of Christianity.

He has to give Himself to me totally or I will reject Him totally. I will never be satisfied with glimpses, with possibilities and probabilities of truth. I must know Him. I must live in His embrace, or I will deny Him as One who does not give all He promises.

Tons of lead are shovelled and smelted in the hope of getting one grain of radium. Years of prison are not too much if once one may have one day with Him. His days are rare, as tungsten and vanadium are rare. His day comes slowly, but when it comes it will compensate for years lost in the darkness of prison cells.

On that day words will no longer mask contrary intentions. Truth will triumph. Human and divine natures will marry, as they are united in Him. We will see things as they are. I will know "the holy thing"; whether this happens in prison or in the bosom of my family will make no difference. Amen.

# MORALS APART FOR THE ELECT

Truth is revolutionary. It even revolutionises its own definition.

One thing comes up again and again. At every interrogation I tell the officer fairy tales: I invent stories to lead him astray. When he asks for concrete details and the names of those with whom I worked underground, I give him the names of people I know are abroad, of some who have died recently, or of their own top stooges within the Church. I usually succeed in making my story plausible, at least for a time, so as to delay a beating until they have checked all the names.

When I return to my cell, I am no longer alone. I have with me a preacher, Mr. Morals, who delivers long sermons about how wrong it is to lie. He quotes Spurgeon to me: "It is never right to do a little wrong to obtain the greatest possible good. Your duty is to do the right: consequences are with God." Or, "I have no right to commit a sin to increase usefulness. I have to be righteous even if it undoes usefulness." I wonder why my Mr. Morals is such a boring preacher, always delivering the same sermon. I would like to hear him speak for a change about how stupid it is to betray brethren to the police while leaving "the consequences to God" – such consequences as hungry wives and orphaned children for whom nobody will care.

The authorities consider it complicity with a counter-revolutionist if you give a piece of bread to the child of a jailed Christian. Mr. Morals teaches that nobody should go against the law of the land, because it is wrong to break laws. The main thing to be concerned about is keeping the magnificent "I" righteous. The conse-quences belong to God. Let Him rain manna again for families of imprisoned Christians.

I have high respect for Mr. Morals. But I believe he delivers his sermon in the wrong place. I would make the proposal that he do some of his preaching to the Communists. Their questioning me about things which are not their concern is surely less moral than my giving deceptive answers.

I am a child of God. In most spheres God's children do not have the same moral standards as common men.

We love our enemies, whereas others consider it right to defeat them. We do the beautiful though unpro-ductive deed: we squander money on costly perfume with which to anoint a Man who will be scourged and crucified tomorrow as a criminal. Others much more practical and better fitted than we to lead charitable, even Christian charitable, institutions condemn such squandering because the money is needed for the poor. Has not God Himself put it in our hearts to provide for them?

We are glad that Jesus is righteous, and we need not try to become righteous ourselves through any deed or attitude of our own.

The others are reasonable, of course. They choose between right and wrong, and they make the proper choice. We believe that *all* things work together for our good – St. Augustine adds: "even our sins" – and we don't make any choices.

Some have before them two ways: one leading to life,

the other to death. We admire them when they step decidedly towards life. But for us death is abolished. The Lord told us, "Whosoever lives and believes in me shall never die" (John 11:26). We are utterly disinterested in this constant oscillation between two paths and hundreds of bypaths. Others exercise their will for good purposes. We don't believe in free will. We believe that right choices as well as their fulfilment are gifts from God, often given to those who seek them least.

I lie to my oppressors. Is truth an absolute obligation? Does the Bible always give the facts as they are? Does it not strain some truth, on occasion even yield truthfulness to love and respect?

I remember a verse from the book of Judges (18:30). I often thought about it, first, when Nazi persecution and, later, when Communist domination obliged us to prevaricate. In it Jonathan, an idolatrous priest in Israel (as a matter of fact the first), is called the son of Gershom. In the Hebrew original, in all the manuscripts, the name Manasseh is written here in a strange manner: מ נ שׁ ה The "n" is suspended above the line to show that it is an addition that veils some secret.

Gershom was a son of Moses. The first idolatrous priest was therefore a grandson of the law-giver. The writer of the sacred book did not wish to do Moses the indignity of publicising the fact. Therefore he changed the name Moses to Manasseh. In Hebrew it took the addition of just one letter. For the few who might understand the subtleties of Scripture and the reason why a letter would be written above the regular line, a reminder of the real fact was left. But the "n" in this position is not the same as a normal "n". A musical note written above a given line can change the whole tune.

Now, was it truth to call Gershom the son of Manasseh when he was actually the son of Moses? Does it please Truth when a great man of God is put to shame? Does she not rather rejoice when she sees respect for such a man?

Does Truth desire only fact, or is she enamoured of other values as well, such as love for the brethren whom I have to protect from arrest? Does Truth consider herself more important than me? Once, using a piece of thread, I cut deeply into my flesh between the toes and did my best to infect the wounds with chalk, in the hope of gaining a better life in the infirmary. Did I offend Truth through this pretence?

The whole matter will have to be elaborated on much further.

The world teaches us to pretend, to be hypocrites. Jesus, too, teaches us to pretend, but with a difference. He does not teach us to show ourselves as we are. When you fast, He says, look like a man who is feasting; when you pray, let people think you are taking a nap; when you give alms, conceal the fact (Matt. 6:1-6,16-18). This is holy deceit. Mr. Morals would condemn this. He would insist on the obligation to tell people exactly what you are doing. He would have rebuked the woman from Tekoah who fabricated a heart-rending story in order to convince David he should forgive his son Absalom, who had greatly sinned (II Sam. 14). Is Truth so adamant in harshness that she would never yield to a fable in order that grace might conquer?

Jesus pretended. When He came to Emmaus, "He made as though he would have gone further," though in reality He wanted to stay with His disciples (Luke 24:28).

It just passes through my mind that if Michelangelo had not started as a genial forger, claiming that a sleeping Cupid he had made was some old Greek sculpture, today we might not have his *Pietà*. People might not have paid any attention to him.

Dare anyone condemn Desdemona, who died with a lie on her lips defending her beloved Othello, who had killed her just because he loved too much and had been the jealous victim of intrigue? Jesus Himself strained the truth at love's behest when He said, "Father, forgive them, for they know not what they do." Every one of them knew how painful crucifixion was.

I believe that all the implications have not yet been drawn from the teachings of the Lord. The simple fact that the business of the merchants of religion doesn't prosper should show us that they don't squeeze out of their merchandise – religion – all the profit it can give. If they were to extract more wisdom from Jesus, they could then glean from the public much more interest in religion.

Jesus has given us His Word – one talent. We should make it ten talents. There are still new worlds to be discovered in the realm of Christian thought. To discover them we have to have courage to leave the secure shore of commonly accepted morals. I, on my part, will "lie" whenever necessary in order to protect my brethren.

# THE ABSOLUTE DUTY OF TRUTHFULNESS

BELOVED BRETHREN AND SISTERS

A Jewess came to a rabbi and told him her troubles and pains. After weeping and sighing for an hour, she finally said, "Rabbi, I feel better now. My headache has disappeared."

"No, my daughter, it has not disappeared," said the rabbi. "Now I have it."

Since the time the Communists took over our country, we have had to start secret Christian activities, first within the Soviet army and then, when the terror began, among Romanians themselves. Secret activity is not possible without a certain amount of lying and deceit. The consciences of many Christians were troubled about this, but instead of living with their troubles, they put them on my shoulders. Their headaches became mine.

Now I lie at every interrogation. Through Morse code the prisoners from the cell nearby tell me that they do the same, but afterwards they feel as if they have sinned greatly and ask me what to do.

I know you all have the same problem, so I will tell you what I think in this matter.

If an authority, the state or your parent acts unjustly, your duty is to resist and oppose the authority. Don't ask me for Bible verses justifying this attitude. There exists a natural law for which no divine revelation is needed. In the Christian era, some men, like Thomas Aquinas for example, justified even the murder of tyrants in extreme cases. (See "Widerstandsrecht" by Ernst Wolf, in the dictionary *Religion in Geschichte und Gegenwart*, 3rd ed., vol. VI.) Luther also recognised this right of resistance.

Do you think your hands remain pure if you refrain from killing the tyrant? He may kill millions of innocents, as did Hitler, and you will be co-responsible if you could have prevented the carnage by destroying the tyrant and his clique of murderers.

The Lutheran bishop Eivind Berggrav of Norway, who sat in prison under the Nazi occupation, later said before the Lutheran World Federation, "If the authority becomes arbitrarily tyrannical, we have a demonic situation, which means a regime which is not submissive to God. It would be a sin to submit to a diabolic power. In such circumstances we have in principle the right to rebellion in one form or another."

If we have the right to resist the tyrant and to deny him the possibility of continuing to live, even more then do we have the right to oppose his inquisitive delving into what he is not entitled to know – the secret activities of the church. We can lie to the Communist persecutor.

Not that it ever becomes right to lie. But it is wrong to prefer your personal purity to responsibility for your neighbour. If you speak the truth, you put your brethren in prison. If you speak the truth, you make the existence of an underground church impossible and deprive whole nations of the Gospel. In order to avoid the guilt of having lied, we take upon ourselves a worse burden. Bonhoeffer said, "True innocence manifests itself just through entering into the communion of error out of love toward another."

We cannot assume the responsibility of telling the

truth to tyrants, because it will help them torture and kill Christians. I will not justify lying either, but I will gladly accept its responsibility before God. I discover that I am able to live with my conscience after having lied.

Here we have a case in which one doesn't have a choice between good and evil, but only between two evils.

Though we sometimes have the duty to lie, still we have the absolute duty of truthfulness. It is a grave sin to trespass against either duty.

The duty to be truthful is obvious.

Christianity presents an incredible message that contradicts the whole of human experience, namely, that a virgin gave birth to the Son of God, that angels appeared and spoke to shepherds regarding the newborn Babe, that stars led wise men to His very house, that Jesus performed miracles as had no man before, that after having died on the cross, He was resurrected bodily and ascended to heaven.

St. Paul, when proclaiming this message to the heathen, offered as proof of its veracity the fact that most of these things regarding Jesus had been predicted by the Jewish prophets. At that time it was no easy matter to become a Christian. It could mean being thrown to the wild beasts. Every man had to think seriously before making such a decision. The most sensible approach would have been to ask the closest Jewish neighbour if his Scriptures had really foretold all these facts about Jesus, to which the answer was invariably, "Jesus was a fake, an impostor, condemned as such by our high priests."

One can see the dilemma of Christianity in the Gospels themselves. The prophet Malachi had predicted that before the appearance of the Messiah, Elijah the prophet would come again. When this objection was brought to Jesus, He answered, "Elijah has come – he is John the Baptist." So priests and Levites were sent to inquire of John the Baptist, who flatly denied that he was Elijah, thus appearing to cancel all the claims of Jesus to be the Anointed.

Under these difficult circumstances it was of the utmost importance that every Christian be an example of truthfulness in private life. His character was the main accreditation of his strange faith. That is why Peter was so harsh to Ananias and Sapphira, who with an outright lie had pretended to be more self-sacrificing Christians than they really were. When discovered, each suffered a shock and died on the spot – as do primitive people today who violate a taboo.

Christians should be truth incarnate, in the full sense of the word. The Greek word for truth is *aletheis,* which means "nothing hidden". The Hebrew word *emet* is composed of the first, middle and last letters of the alphabet, indicating that truth exists only when it is all of a piece from beginning to end, without any alteration or misrepresentation. Every half-truth is a full lie.

But somehow life leaves us all forsworn. I don't know a man who would never act or pretend. I can understand Ananias and Sapphira. They loved the Lord and His company. They wanted to belong and for this sacrificed the greatest part of their substance. They also reserved something for themselves because they sensed rightly that the first love of Christians would not last. Very soon financial quarrels would arise among them (Acts 6), and they might find themselves with nothing in their old age. Their thoughts were much too complicated to be told to enthusiastic apostles who had given away everything. Curiously, the name Sapphira means in Hebrew "calculation".

Peter, who had himself pretended to be a hero on the night of Jesus' betrayal, was harsh to them. Some time later, he was rebuked publicly by Paul for pretending to be faithful to the Jewish religion. John, the apostle, was very nearly befriended by the high priest, who hated Jesus. For such treatment he must have indulged in some prevarication.

Life is impossible without the theatre of courtesy, gentleness, good manners – the niceties which never correspond entirely to the state of the heart. So, then, absolute truthfulness is necessary and absolute truthfulness is impossible. How can we resolve this problem?

In a sense, every man's life is a pretence because to be an "I", a separate entity, is a lie. Jesus said you must deny yourself (Luke 9:23), that is, acknowledge the unreality of the "I", which is no more than the point of convergence of a multitude of hereditary features, of social influences, of the impact of good and evil spirits, of works of nature, and so on. A Hindu once asked a child, "Break open that fruit and what will you see in it?"

"Seeds," came the reply.

"Break open the seeds and what do you see?"

"Nothing."

The Hindu said, "When there is a nothing, a tree grows."

Your pretence will cease only with your denying the "I". Then truth will grow on your boughs.

Constantine the Great suffered terrible remorse about having killed his son. He asked all kinds of heathen priests and philosophers if there were forgiveness for him. He received only negative replies. Then he asked the Christians, and they told him how easy it is to receive forgiveness. On whom does the sin lie? On the "I", but the lie of its existence can easily be detected. The "I" can be denied. Then only Christ remains. He gladly bears the responsibility of everything which has ever happened. He is the Lamb which has taken away the sin of the world. He said, "I am the truth."

Therefore, when the "I" is denied, only the one incomparable, indivisible Truth remains, and lies will disappear. To whom should *the* Truth lie? Before whom does He ever have to play-act if He is all? Jesus is the intellectual and spiritual expression of reality. He is for me the only "I". If He is my all in all, the truth embodied in Him will accredit itself. It is His concern, not mine.

Jesus is a Saviour to the uttermost. Thus He saves me from the constant nagging worries about whether or not I have spoken or served the truth. I leave Him this burden, too.

A Russian brother told us about an occurrence in Odessa.

The underground church wanted to baptise a group of some twenty individuals. They considered a fish-hatchery at the edge of town to be the best place. The old caretaker was known to go to bed early. Fish would not create a disturbance. There was plenty of water. So the baptism took place there.

The next day, the old caretaker went to the president of the Soviet and asked to be given another job. "Why?" he was asked. "You will never find a more suitable place to work."

"No, I will never go back. The hatchery is haunted." And he explained: "Last night I saw some twenty beings who looked like men, but in reality they were something else. Beauty that was not earthly radiated from everyone. They sang songs entirely unlike anything we sing in our pubs. Then they entered the water one by one, and when they came out of it, I had no doubts any more. They were unearthly. I could not explain who they were. But I won't go back."

The caretaker saw things better than we do when we have a baptism. He observed that we are moved into an entirely new sphere – that of the children of God. The difference between a child of God and a man is much greater than that between a man and an ape.

We are partakers of the divine nature (II Pet. 1:4) and belong to the world which gives commandments, not to that which strives to obey them. Non-Christians who acknowledge the obligation to be truthful find themselves the victims of inner tension because their fallen nature keeps them from adequately fulfilling their duty. As Christians we don't have the duty of truthfulness: we have its character. We speak it as it is given to us. We can have the full confidence that what we speak is truly what God wishes the other man to know.

We don't have to calculate like Ananias and Sapphira what to give and what to say in order to justify ourselves. Everything has been given. We are just, through the blood of Christ, and never need any further justification. Saving truth emanates spontaneously from our renewed heart.

As children of God we live in a mysterious sphere. Our father in faith is Abraham, who was ordered by God to commit what is considered among men to be a horrible crime: to kill his own son. He was prepared to do so, and he was praised for his willingness.

All human moral standards cease to be valid here. We have as our God a Being who not only bruised His Son, but found pleasure in doing so (Isaiah 53:10). If the salvation of mankind cost so much, the Father paid the price willingly. Why should this Father object to letting me, another child of His, purvey to my interrogators what humans would call an untruth, in order to save the underground church, His messengers of salvation? I have no "I". Let Him decide. Amen.

# THE SPACES IN THE BIBLE

DEAR BRETHREN AND SISTERS

Until I went to prison I thought I believed that the Bible was the Word of God. If anyone had asked me if I believed the *whole* Bible to be His Word, without hesitation I would have answered, "Yes."

I realise now that I was mistaken. I had only *thought* I believed so. The Bible consists of white sheets of paper (in former times, of parchments), on which are imprinted or inscribed black letters. Around these characters, between the lines and words and in the margins, is a considerable mass of blank space, perhaps even more than that occupied by words. The Bible could not exist without this empty space. Does it also belong to the Word of God, or is it sheer nothing? Does a "nothing" exist? Something that is cannot be nothing. The figure zero never occurs in the Bible.

Is it not possible that the empty spaces in the Bible – its silences – are at least as important as its words? One can find contradictions and debatable matters in the words of the Bible, but nobody can contradict the silence of the depths of its blank spaces.

We are told that when the Lord Jesus was brought to the temple at the age of twelve He amazed the priests with the questions He asked and the answers He gave. I am not very much interested in the amazement of the priests. I would have preferred to know what Jesus' questions and answers were. They cannot be found in the black letters of the Gospel. But keep quiet and you will find them. They are contained in the blank space. In the quiet of a subterranean solitary cell I can read them.

In the prologue to his Gospel St. Luke writes that he first inquired diligently of eyewitnesses about all the episodes in the life of Jesus. In the course of his inquiries he must have gone to the house of Lazarus to ask about the visits of Jesus in Bethany. Martha told him that she had had a quarrel with her sister in the presence of Jesus. Luke may have considered the matter a trifle, he noted it. Then he asked Mary to tell her side of the story. She answered, "Martha chided me for not helping out in the kitchen, but I preferred to sit a couple of hours at the feet of Jesus and listen to Him. I did not wish to lose a word of what He had to say."

"You are the person I need," St. Luke would have exclaimed. "Please tell me the teachings that Jesus gave on that evening."

She surely would have answered, but nowhere do we find this information in Luke's books. We are only told that Mary listened to Him and that Jesus praised her for choosing the good part.

That is to say, we do not find Mary's memories about Jesus' talk in the black letters of the Bible. They are in the white space between chapters 10 and 11 of St. Luke.

There have been centuries of debate about the question of whether the bread and wine in holy communion really become the body and blood of the Saviour. But one thing is above debate: paper takes on a different value when the Bible is printed on it. That is why multitudes of Jews and Christians who have never read the Bible can be seen kissing it in synagogues and Orthodox churches. If the Word can become flesh, sanctifying the womb of the virgin who bore Him, then the written Word can also give exceptional value to sheets of paper on which it is inscribed.

Even stones can become holy. Soviet soldiers told us about the church of the Holy Blood of Christ in Leningrad, closed by the authorities, whose walls bear hundreds of inscriptions: "God, give me love", "Lord, give me happiness", and others like these. Why do people feel instinctively that the right place to inscribe such requests is on the wall of what was once a church? Is it not like any other wall? Why do Jews travel clear around the world just to pray at the wailing wall in Jerusalem? Could they not do the same thing leaning on the wall of their kitchens?

I know a good portion of the Bible by heart and "read" whole chapters from memory in my prison cell, but it is not at all like having the real Book before me. Its very paper is a marvel. In every fibre there are as many atoms as there are drops of water in the ocean or blades of grass on the whole earth. And the atoms are constituted of smaller particles. Electrons travel at the speed of 10,000 miles per second. While I read a page of the Bible, they will have travelled the distance from Bucharest to Tokyo countless times, while keeping the Word of God inviolate. The electrons constituting my own eyes also travel, perhaps lovingly chasing those of the Bible. The piece of paper is not dull and dead. It is one of God's mysteries; it is a cyclone of energy.

Paper has a dramatic history of its own. It was once a tree in the forest. Sunbeams played through its branches, birds made their nests in it and chirped, ants and insects scurried over its bark, lovers kissed each other in its shadow. Then rude men felled the tree. Seeing the wretchedness of slave labourers, it would not have known for whom to weep. It could almost forget its own tragedy at the sight of prisoners who were hungry, dirty, poorly clothed, unskilled in this work, often injured, and who were forced to do this hard work under the surveillance of wardens with whips. A part of the tree became paper on which pornography or hate literature was printed. A part of it became Scripture. There exists a chosen people of God; there exists the elect of God in every nation; there are chosen walls; there exist chosen sheets of paper.

Mad thoughts? Perhaps. Which thoughts of a prisoner are not mad? Many of my ideas are foolish, although frenzy has not completely seized me yet. Otherwise I would not know that my ideas are foolish and I would not feel unhappy.

My observations about the travel of electrons applies to all paper, not only to that used for printing Bibles. True, but it is only through reading Holy Scripture that one gains an awesome respect for matter. Materialists do not love matter. They have no sense of its "earnest expectation" (Rom. 8:19), do not sympathise with its "bondage of corruption" (Rom. 8:21).

Listen! Maybe I will hear the ringing of church bells outside. It is a Sunday morning. Bells. Men have made brass express adoration for God. Materialists cannot make matter radiate the praises of atheism, of the nonexistence of God. The Word becomes not only flesh but matter. Jesus Himself as an incipient embryo was matter before becoming flesh.

The atom is mysterious; the world is mysterious; the Bible is also mysterious. If its meaning were plain, it would be the work of men. But it comes from another sphere. Let us take advantage of what is clear in Scripture and trust for the rest. One day we will be in the light, and then we shall no longer see "through a glass, darkly" (1 Cor. 13:12).

Never stop at the black letters of the Bible. If you were to ask me which Bible verses support me the most today, my answer would be, "The Bible verses which comfort me most are two verses which are not in the Bible."

First, I am happy that the Bible never mentions Jesus' asking anybody what sins he had committed, how many, of what gravity, under what circumstances, with what complicity. He met sinners and told them, "Be of good cheer, son or daughter, your sins are forgiven."

Second, what I appreciate is that the Bible records no instance in which anyone apologised or asked Jesus for forgiveness during His earthly life. On the last evening before His crucifixion the disciples had forsaken Him and one had denied Him. Afterwards, when they met their resurrected Lord, they should at least have said, "I'm sorry." But whoever looked into the face of Jesus saw so much kindness, so much love, such a willingness to forgive, that he knew there was no need to ask.

And so I say, read not only what the Bible records in black on white, but read its white spaces. Listen to its silences. They are eloquent. You are not asked what sins you have committed, nor are you commanded to utter long prayers of repentance. Rather, believe that His blood *has* cleansed you of all your sins, and rejoice.

Where we don't understand a part of the Bible, it is the simplest thing to say humbly, "I can't understand," and to reflect that we are acquainted with only the fringes of reality. The Author of the Bible can be trusted.

The proof of God's existence is that He has produced the Bible, and the proof of the Bible is that so marvellous a book could have been produced only by God. Communists and some scientists claim that the world was not created by God. And if they were right? There would be reason enough to adore Him if He had produced only the Bible.

A man who has lost, in addition to his beloved ones, all his belongings, his health, his reputation, his liberty, or even just a needle, must seek these things in the Bible. He will surely find more than he has lost – the conviction of the irrelevance of the things lost. One thing is needed. Following the Bible, you will have chosen the good part. And you will find *the* Beloved. Amen.

# SINS ARE SO SMALL TO HIM

BELOVED BRETHREN AND SISTERS

There is an abyss of sins in every one of us, the muck of generations.

On a certain Sunday I had preached twice and by evening was tired and in need of rest. But I felt a strong impulse to go to the pub which was just opposite my parsonage. When I told my wife about it, she objected vigorously.

"You spoke twice today against drinking, and now all the neighbours will see you going to have a drink. You can't do such a thing. You'll be slandered."

"Come with me," I replied, "so they will slander us both."

When we entered the pub, I understood why I had been brought here. In the midst stood a Russian captain with his finger on the trigger of a revolver, threatening to shoot everybody. He was drunk and had asked for more liquor. It had been refused him, and now he was terribly angry. People had hidden behind the bar and under tables. They could not parley with him, not knowing Russian. I could speak the language.

When I asked him what was happening, he quieted down a little and explained his demand. I assured him that I would take care of it if only he would keep quiet. I went to the pub owner and promised him that my wife and I would sit with the captain and entertain him so

46

there would be no further trouble. "Give him one bottle more."

The pub owner was so happy he exclaimed, "Pastor, you have saved my life! I will always remain grateful. Henceforth in my bar you can drink as much as you like free of charge."

The Russian captain, my wife, and I sat down at a table. A bottle of wine and three glasses were served. He was polite. He filled the glasses. My wife did not drink and I did not drink, but he showed courtesy. He would empty all three glasses. He was drunk, but he was used to drinking. He could reason and understand.

So while he drank, I told him the old, old story about the Son of God, who came down from heaven, was born of a virgin in a stable, taught love, led a life of sorrows, in the end was crucified for our sins, was raised from the dead, ascended to heaven, and is preparing for every repentant sinner who puts his confidence in Him an eternal abode in bliss. He listened attentively while drinking.

When I finished, he said, "Now that I know who you are, I will tell you who I am. I am an Orthodox priest. When, under Stalin, 80,000 priests were killed, I was terribly frightened. And so I accepted the offer which the Communists made to become an atheist lecturer.

"Though believing in God, I agreed to go from town to town, from village to village, to convince people that there is no God, no Christ and no eternal life. I have destroyed the faith of many people, including my former parishioners. I could not conquer fear. My punishment from God has been that with this hand with which I gave holy communion before, I have had to shoot Christians who refused to serve in the Red Army.

"And now I drink and drink to forget what I have

done, but I cannot forget. Waiter, bring another bottle."

Silently I adored the Holy Spirit, who brings us to the right place at the right time.

I asked the captain, "Do you still know the creed?"

He vaguely remembered it. Many years had passed since he had said it last.

So I began to recite in Russian, "I believe in one God, the Father almighty," and so on until I came to the words, "I believe in the remission of sins." I asked him, "Do you believe in this article of the creed?"

"I made it clear that I believe the whole Christian faith," he answered. "It was only fear that made me deny it."

I insisted, "Do you believe in the remission of sins?"

"Yes."

I pressed hard, "Do you believe in the remission of *your* sins?"

"Oh, no!" he shouted. "My sins have amounted to crimes and have been far too many."

"The creed does not state that only small and few offences are forgiven, but everything, all sins, without counting the number or looking at the size. When John the Baptist saw the Lord Jesus, he said, 'Behold the Lamb of God, which taketh away the sin of the *world*.' If you alone had committed all the murders, thefts, lies, perjuries, and adulteries committed by all mankind from the beginning but now believe in Jesus, behold, He is the Lamb of God who takes away the sins of the world. Do you believe in the remission of *your* sins?"

In tears, the officer repeated again and again, "I believe in the remission of *my* sins." Jesus had performed a masterwork. He had found not a lost sheep, but a lost shepherd.

I never saw this captain again. It was wartime. On the

next day he had gone further towards the front with his regiment. What did he do afterwards?

On the first day of her conversion the Samaritan woman brought the population of a whole town to Christ. What did she do later? Did her enthusiasm last? Did she continue to win multitudes as in the beginning, or did she pass into the arms of another husband? Jesus praised a Roman centurion for having faith such as one could not find even in Israel. What deeds did he perform with this faith? Or, once satisfied with the miracle he had expected, did he return to his duty, which was training soldiers to kill? Zaccheus promised to return everything he had extorted and give fourfold to everyone he had defrauded. Did he keep his promise?

I like Ezekiel 20:3: "As I live, saith the Lord God, I will not be inquired of by you." He wanted us to know a part of the story. Let it be enough for us. This captain, the Samaritan woman, the centurion, and Zaccheus all had *one* good moment when they put their trust in Jesus. The rest is not our business.

The Russian captain had been cleansed. What looked to me and to him like a mountain of sin seemed to Jesus, who sees things from highest heaven, an insignificant mound.

In Old Testament times the Jews went astray by believing in Moloch. In Hebrew, Moloch means "the king who has reigned". Too often we have our souls fixed upon ugly events in the past. Christians believe in Jimloh, "the King who will reign". Worshippers of Jimloh believe that the past is forgiven and also repaired. Christians also believe in a holiness towards which we evolve. "He which hath begun a good work in you," writes the apostle Paul, "will perform it until the day of Jesus Christ" (Phil. 1:6).

The Hebrews used the word *hatath* for a sin of a man

towards a fellow man, and *asham* for the sin of a man towards God, such as breaking the Sabbath or disobeying some ritual law. But *asham* meant also the restitution which a thief had to make for what he had stolen. In Isaiah 53:10, it is said that Jesus will make his soul an *asham*, which means not only an offering for sin, but also a restitution for it. In some mysterious ways the Almighty will restore all I have done wrong.

In Shakespeare's *Hamlet*, a wretched Claudius seeks to pray:

> O my offence is rank, it smells to heaven!
> It has the primal eldest curse upon 't;
> A brother's murder. Pray can I not.
> Though inclination be as sharp as will,
> My stronger guilt defeats my strong intent,
> And, like a man to double business bound,
> I stand in pause where I shall first begin,
> And both neglect ...
> My fault is past. But, O, what form of prayer
> Can serve my turn? 'Forgive me my foul murder?'
> That cannot be, since I am still possess'd
> Of those effects for which I did the murder,
> My crown, mine own ambition, and my queen.
> May one be pardon'd and retain th' offence?

I reply: "Claudius, I can give you the answer. We can now speak freely with each other, both belonging to the same unreal world. You were buried after you died. I am buried alive. It doesn't make much difference. We can communicate. Yes, Claudius, you can be forgiven too, though you can repair nothing. If you were now to send away your wife whom you obtained in a criminal manner, you would bring upon her new unhappiness and new temptations. If you renounced the crown, one who never prays might pick it up. Leave things as they are and believe in Jesus, the *asham*, the restitution."

You can begin every day anew, unburdened by the past. And don't be afraid today of repeating the same old wrongs. Rather, be pleasantly surprised if it happens otherwise. God knows that your piano is bad and that you cannot make it produce good melodies. Only your inner state counts. God judges you according to your will only. Would Menuhin's concert be as pleasant to the ear if he played a gypsy's violin instead of the Stradivarius he uses? God looks at what you will, not at how much you can fulfil.

Your sins are remitted. Amen.

# MEASURE IN DELICACY

DEAR BRETHREN AND SISTERS

Mary Stuart accidentally stepped on the toes of the henchman when she was on the scaffold. It is said that her last words were, "I beg your pardon, sir executioner." She was a queen. Her good breeding was instinctive.

Likewise Christians, children of the heavenly King, show meekness when they are ill-used.

Christians simply love and shine. They do so even when, like their Master, they wear a crown of thorns and have in their hand a reed for a sceptre.

Believers also show kindness to those doomed by God.

God said to Moses, "Rise ye up, take your journey, and pass over the river Arnon: behold, I have given into thine hand Sihon the Amorite, king of Heshbon, and his land: begin to possess it, and contend with him in battle. This day will I begin to put the dread of thee and the fear of thee upon the nations that are under the whole heaven, who shall hear report of thee, and shall tremble, and be in anguish because of thee." And Moses "sent messengers out of the wilderness of Kedemoth unto Sihon king of Heshbon with words of peace" (Deut. 2:24–26).

Moses had been given the order to destroy a king. But as in the case of Pharaoh, God allowed Moses to proffer peace and an amicable agreement to the heathen king.

It is permissible to send words of peace even to those utterly rejected by the Creator.

The Christian is engaged in warfare as long as he lives on this earth. But his role can be compared to that of a military physician. He has to give medicine and comfort to the wounded on both sides.

Such Christian delicacy has produced changes in the heathen world.

Mahatma Gandhi wrote, "It was the New Testament which really awakened me to the rightness and value of passive resistance and love towards one's enemies." In 1908, when he was almost murdered by a Moslem, he did not prosecute him nor give evidence against him. This forgiven murderer became a disciple of Gandhi.

A similar story is told about the Christian Mrs. Rathenau. Her husband, finance minister of Germany, had been killed by a Nazi only for the crime of having Jewish blood. Mrs. Rathenau cared for the murderer in prison and defended him. During the war, this murderer became a leader of the Gestapo in Marseilles. He atoned for the evil done in the past by helping multitudes of Jews escape, with the result that in the end he was hanged.

Edmund Campion, English Jesuit, betrayed by a Catholic turned Protestant, was thrice tortured on the rack. Then he was sentenced to be hanged, drawn and quartered. A *Te Deum* was sung at this occasion. But the traitor had come to death row asking forgiveness. Campion gave it. He helped his denunciator escape the pursuers who sought revenge: he gave him a letter to a German nobleman recommending him for service.

These are the attitudes God likes. They are at the opposite pole to that of the Spanish patriot Narvaez who, when asked on his deathbed by his confessor if he had forgiven all his enemies, replied, "Father, I have no enemies. I've shot them all."

But there is a limit to Christian forbearance and charity. In the end, Moses killed Sihon and his subjects because they were not responsive to delicacy. At times we have to have measure in love. One single devil whom we have pitied can destroy a paradise.

One day of softness and a nation can lose overnight happy institutions built up through generations of struggle.

Do not think it virtue to be delicate only. When occasion demands, tell a devil in high position that he is a devil.

The good pastor is the one who has the proper measure even in love.

We read in Revelation 20: 3 that after the Devil has fulfilled a thousand years of prison, he will be given a period of amnesty for "a little season". But once free, he will start his wicked deeds again, gathering together the nations of earth for another world war, which only God will bring to a fiery end.

Jesus is full of grace. One cannot find the right expression in English for saying how full of grace He is. In Hebrew the singular "mercy" does not exist. The word is plural: *rahamim* – "mercies." Nobody can obtain from God only one mercy, because He has only indivisible bushels of it. In the New Testament, the corresponding Greek work *oiktirmos* is also used frequently in the plural form.

Shakespeare wrote, Troubles come not singly, but in battalions. Likewise, a sin never occurs alone but in the company of many others. And graces abound even more. But a plurality of mercies does not mean that there is no limit to them. The universe is constructed mathematically. We might not know how many stars there are, but there is a certain definite number. Jesus taught us to forgive much, and He told us exactly, mathematically, how much to forgive. He taught us not to remit indefinitely, but exactly 490 times (Matt. 18:22). Where there are figures, we have a very exact teaching.

Jesus was not full of grace alone, but of "grace and truth" (John 1:14). Now, John thought in Hebrew. In Hebrew the letter "v", which stands for "and" is part of the following word. John wrote "andtruth" as a single word. Grace which is not limited by the supreme interest that truth should triumph is a dangerous fancy.

A man can love many things. He can have a passion for only one. Results are achieved only if that man desires one thing exclusively and does not squander his energies simultaneously on a hundred other things. I admire the Communists for concentrating all their efforts on the fulfilling of their supreme passion. Our passion is the triumph of Christ, the establishment of His kingdom, which necessarily includes the overthrow of everything which opposes it. We have a place for delicacy, for genuine love towards the enemy, but only in the measure to which this would not defeat our main purpose. To love the enemy so much as to enable him to overcome us is idiocy.

I love my enemy, but I do not forget that while I spend my time preparing a series of good deeds for him, he prepares weapons to destroy my church. He might strike quickly and unexpectedly while I indulge in sentiments of love.

In extreme cases in the heat of battle, the military doctor might be forced to shoot. He also is a warrior. We Christians have to adopt the military mentality, remembering how many are the metaphors about warfare in the New Testament: "the weapons of our warfare" (II Cor. 10:4); "Put on the whole armour of

God... we wrestle... having on the breastplate... taking the shield... the helmet... the sword of the Spirit" (Eph. 6:11-17); "Let us put on the armour of light" (Rom. 13:12).

In war I don't admire so much the hero who dies for his fatherland as the one who lets the enemy die for *his*. A live hero is worth more than a dead one. Truth is exclusive. With Christ as our Commander, right is on our side, we must conquer.

We allow ourselves gestures of delicacy, we nurture love for all men, including our enemies, with one limitation: we must be victorious. Every gentle act which does not hinder this is welcome.

I remember the first Soviet officer I met. I asked him if he believed in God. I would not have minded if he had said "No". Freedom is given to every man to say "Yes" or "No" even to God. But he gave me the most amazing answer: "We have no order to believe. If we get such an order, we will."

I had met the typical Soviet man, a being who has been robbed of the highest gift made by God to man: to be an individual in his own right. He had been changed into a robot who waited for orders about what faith to embrace or reject. The Communists don't allow any sphere in which the individual is free. One has to be a Marxist even in art and science. Because of Einstein's discoveries, the universe we live in bears his name. Yet his book *The World As I See It* is forbidden in Communist countries because he expresses his belief in God – an incredible irony.

Such a regime has to disappear. Brethren, do everything you can to this end. Don't ask, "What can I, a single man, do?" If everyone asked himself this, no collective good would ever be achieved. The regime *must* disappear.

Therefore, love the Communists and be gentle towards them only in the measure to which this does not conflict with the main purpose. Robots must be changed into men again. Christ must be proclaimed and accepted freely. His kingdom must come.

After having prayed and fasted many years, the fathers in the desert – the first generation of monks who fled to the wilderness of Thebaide from the corruption of the church which had become a state institution in the fourth century – gathered for counselling. St. Anthony the Great asked them, "Let everyone say which Christian virtue he considers the highest."

A few arose immediately and said, "Love." Others said, "Humility." Some said, "Obedience." Some put "Silence" on the highest level. In the end they asked St. Anthony, who had listened attentively to their debate, which in his opinion was the highest virtue, and this would prevail.

"All these virtues you have mentioned are excellent," St. Anthony said, "but the highest is to have in all things the right measure."

Measure therefore your delicacy.

The same Bible that teaches love and gentleness also forbids one even to greet certain men (II John 10, 11). Saying "Good morning" to such men (whom John describes) makes one a partaker of his evil deeds. John the Evangelist is said to have fled naked from a public bath when he saw Cerintus, the heretic, entering. He did not wish to remain under the same roof with one who taught false doctrine.

Delicacy, then, to a point. But uncompromising staunchness in matters of truth. Amen.

# UNREACHABLE HEIGHTS

DEAR BRETHREN AND SISTERS

One of Jesus' promises has surely remained unfulfilled. He said that if we have faith as large as a mustard seed, we will be able to move mountains. I don't expect so much. But again and again I have ordered a mere prison wall to move, and it has not. It is written, "This stone . . . has heard" (Joshua 24:27). Why then did it not move? Is my faith smaller than a mustard seed? But what about the faith of my fellow-sufferers? Around me are important saints and bishops. None of them can move even a wall, much less a mountain.

And if one promise of Jesus does not hold true, what should we think about all the others? I shout again and again in my folly, "Wall, move! Wall, move!" It does not move.

For a while I forgot where I was. I shouted loudly. The wardens heard and gathered around my door to ask what was happening. They mocked me when I explained.

I fell down on my bed in despair, overcome with the realisation that I was still in prison. And – far worse – that my faith in His Word was gone.

But slowly I quieted down. A thought flashed through my mind. How is it that I could be so mad? Jesus had been very explicit. If we have only a little faith, the size of a mustard seed, then we will move mountains. But a great God gives a great faith, not tiny coins. Just as the great steel demolition hammers used in industry to smash concrete walls are no good for cracking a nut, so our God-given faith, which is huge, cannot move mere mountains. The only requisite for removing mountains is mundane faith in engineering technology. Our God-given faith does greater things. We leap upon the mountains, we skip upon the hills (Song of Solomon 2:8).

Eventually we may tire of such things. For if I jump over a mountain, I only come upon another valley which lies in the shadow of death. Our great God provides power for more than this.

The woman in Revelation was given the wings of a great eagle (Rev. 12:14) and could soar over mountain peaks. Whitefield entered in his diary, "I prayed God this day that God might make me an extraordinary Christian." And his prayer was fulfilled.

Nothing of the ordinary Christian life fully satisfies us, not even the gift of snowy whiteness of soul or joy like that of a marriage feast. Whiteness and marriage belong to the created world. We are partakers of the divine nature, and nothing less than oneness with the Creator can satisfy us.

Remain, prison walls, where you are. We fly towards the Infinite.

We can do so because for this we were born.

A whole life's work will not enrich a proletarian. Neither will revolutions. With very few exceptions, only that man is rich who is born rich. Those who have acquired wealth are often too old or jaded to enjoy it. A good birth, therefore, is more advantageous than a lifetime of hard work. As for us, everything is ours without working. For as the eagle takes its little ones on its wings, so does our God.

Remain, Communist world and Christian world, where you are. I hate the first. I am sceptical about the second. The old story repeats itself. Men of one and the same generation were pagans under Diocletian, Christians under the emperor Constantine because it became the fashion, Arians under Constantius because the king, a tyrant, thus decreed, and apostates in Julian's time because the emperor willed it. Then they returned to Christianity in Jovinian's time.

In my generation, men of our province, Transylvania, started out as loyal subjects of the Hapsburgs but afterward became loyal subjects of the Romanian kings. All those who had sworn faith to King Charles II were forsworn when he was deposed. These same men became legionnaires, then anti-legionnaires when the former were overthrown by Antonescu.

Bishops who would have refused ordination of men who did not want to swear loyalty to King Michael swore loyalty to the Republic when the king was overthrown. A mass of Christians, headed by their bishops and denominational leaders, passed to the side of the Reds. The same patriarch who had called upon us to fight the Bolshevik dragon celebrated a thanksgiving liturgy for the advent of power of this dragon. Many have left their faith altogether.

Why should I remain in this world, in this Communist state, in this Christianity, in a prison cell or even at liberty? God has smuggled through the locked door of my cell the wings of a great eagle. I fly to the Infinite. Nothing less will do.

I consider myself as having attained nothing while anything remains unattained.

Can it be that when I have reached a certain height I will fall? The devil is a good hunter and hurls darts that travel far.

The Lord has told us that not a sparrow falls to the

ground without our Father (Matt. 10:29). I have seen many sparrows that have fallen. I even saw one eaten by a cat. The Father willed that this sparrow should have a tragic end. I may fall, too. But if, in the future, sins destroy me after I "have tasted of the heavenly gift, and [been] made partaker of the Holy Ghost" (Heb. 6:4), others will learn from my failure and will do better. So I will have served, notwithstanding.

I don't accept as my religion anything apart from union between bride and bridegroom. All other religion is fornication, idolatry. I will soar where the Truth, which sages on earth call by different names, is one.

It is not a certainty that I will fall, though many have. By His grace I may reach the height. Others have; why not I?

I am in the communion of saints. Welcome, St. Catherine, to my prison cell. You were very unlike me. At the age of six, when I had the first vision of what I know now to have been the devil, which shattered my life, you saw Christ blessing you from heaven and apostles standing around you. While I in my youth indulged in gross sins, you had a plank for a bed, a wooden log as a pillow, and you spent your time in prayer and mortification. And you arrived at a spiritual marriage. Christ placed a ring on your finger.

But you give the impression of not seeing any difference between you and me. Maybe I am wrong, but you seem to have even a touch of envy as you look at me. Jesus said, "To whom little is forgiven, the same loves little" (Luke 7:47). Except for original sin, there must have been almost nothing to be forgiven you. You have travelled another way, but you assure me – and must have assured Jesus – that, although God has preserved you from much actual sin, you still love Him passionately.

How beautiful it is to commune with you. You speak

my language. You were a prisoner too. I sit in a Communist cell. You spent almost all your life in the inner cell of your soul. You were like all the brides of Jesus, "a garden enclosed . . . a spring shut up, a fountain sealed" (Song of Solomon 4:12).

You too know actual prison life well. "Don't be surprised at my visit. I had the habit of visiting prisons from an early age," you said, reminding me how you attended barbarous executions when young in order to comfort the condemned and their relatives.

I know from the Bible that "we are compassed about" with a great "cloud of witnesses," men and women who have given their lives to Jesus, the real saints (Heb. 12:1), but I imagine that, when they make themselves felt so clearly, they must have a certain precise intention. Before asking St. Catherine about it, I tried to find out something from her that interested me most:

"I have brought to Christ a Jew of over ninety. He told me once that in a dream he had asked Jesus to show him my place in heaven. He got no reply. It is said that you have an exceptional sensibility about the inner state of a man. You can 'smell' his integrity or corruption. I vacillate between states in which I feel myself a beloved child of God and other states in which I want to warn all men not to be at the last judgment as I am. Can you tell me the truth about me?"

She smiled and remained silent.

But I could remember clearly what I had read about her criticising the luxuries of the church of her time. Still, I had not changed my style of life, which surely had been luxurious compared to that of many of my colleagues.

"Catherine, you have changed much. In times past, you did not mince words even when speaking to a pope. You wrote to Gregory XI, 'Don't be a boy, be a man. If you are not willing to use your power for cauterising the ills of the church, it would be better for you to resign.' You had called cardinals 'poor mean knights, afraid even of their own shadows, poisoned with self-love'. How is it that you don't give me a word of reproof, if you have come for this? Well, it is probably because I am neither a pope nor a cardinal.

"You have come just to remind me that a Christian can reach seemingly unattainable heights. You could write to Charles V, 'When will you fulfil the will of God and me to make peace?' Your will and God's had become identical. You could speak about the two in the same breath.

"Silently you have fulfilled the purpose of your coming. I receive the gift, and now I will soar on eagle's wings."

How beautiful is the communion of the saints. You enjoy it only when you accept its full silence, a silence like that of this prison cell, interrupted only from time to time by the agonised cry of someone who is suffering. I see something with my spiritual eyes. I wonder if I have seen. Perhaps there are drugs in my food. I see so many mad fancies. I had known a madman in an asylum, one of the best men I ever knew. He was a religious maniac. He often saw St. Birgit. He had painted her image on the wall of his cell. I asked him what she told him in their encounters. He smiled, forlorn. That was all. Well, he was mad.

But mad or not, what does it matter to me? I wish to arrive at the spiritual marriage at least in my fantasy. Madmen who dream of being Napoleon or some saint feel so happy. Marriage with Jesus must be glorious even if it is only in imagination.

An ancient sage sent his son to a Bible teacher. When the boy returned, the father asked him, "What did you learn?" The son told him all the subject matter. "This is nothing," the father replied. "Go and learn more." The son returned one year later. This time he boasted of having learned other disciplines. The father sent him back a second time. When the son returned again, his face shone. The father embraced him. "You knew theology before. Now you know God."

If my marriage to Jesus is only imaginary, perhaps men around me will only imagine that my face shines, but this will make them seek God as if I had been truly glorified.

So for their sake, I love you, heights. I come! Amen.

# TAKING HOLD OF THE SKIRT
# OF A JEW

DEAR BRETHREN AND SISTERS IN CHRIST

Today a particularly offensive upstart gave me a beating with special mention that my being a Jew played a role in my torment. Heavy chains were put on my legs.

Sometimes I have slept off the beating. It is amazing how well one can sleep in spite of the pain. Sometimes I have whistled. Now I remember a Bible verse: "It shall come to pass, that ten men shall take hold out of all languages of the nations, even shall take hold of the skirt of him that is a Jew, saying, We will go with you: for we have heard that God is with you" (Zech. 8:23).

This is God's promise. But men take hold of the skirt of a Jew for different purposes. Mrs. Potiphar "caught [Joseph] by his garment, saying, Lie with me" (Gen. 39:12). Many catch Jews by their garments to have them as business partners. Here in prison they catch you by your skirt and hold you fast during a beating. The Communists mistreat everybody, but Jewish prisoners always get a double beating.

Some of the officers of the Secret Police are turncoats, former members of anti-Semitic organisations, who give vent to their real feelings when they have a Jewish prisoner in their hands, to compensate for being compelled to stand at attention before the Red high

officials of Jewish descent. The Jewish officers of the
Secret Police also take pains to exhibit special harshness
towards Jewish prisoners to avoid the suspicion that
they are partial.

I am Jewish. I had to suffer under the Nazis for the
double crime of being both a Jew and a Christian. Now
it happens all over again. What is it with us Jews? Even
when I was a child, teachers and pupils hit me for being
Jewish. What is it with me?

Are we the withered boughs that have to be broken
off, as Isaiah prophesied (27:11)? After the Nazi defeat,
Christians felt themselves in bad company when
accusing us and abandoned the charge that we
sentenced Jesus to death. Many church leaders change
their opinions as the political winds blow. Those who
have cooperated most with the anti-Semitic killers to
avenge our ancestors' crucifixion of Christ now assure
everyone that Jews were no guiltier in this tragedy than
the Romans. They ignore the fact that the Jews had
prophecies about the coming of Christ, which the
heathen did not have. Ezekiel says about the Jews,
"When they entered unto the heathen, whither they
went, they profaned my holy name" (Ezek. 36:20).
St. Paul's rebuke is also justified: "The name of God
is blasphemed among the Gentiles through you"
(Rom. 2:24).

But I belong to another category of Jew. At Golgotha
the Jewish people divided into two parts: those who had
asked for His death, and those who wept for Him and
eventually constituted the first church. I belong to those
about whom Jesus said, "Salvation is of the Jews" (John
4:22).

Why do they take hold of my garment, too, only to
beat me? What is it with the Jewish question?

Hegel said there was one thing his philosophy could

not explain and that was Israel. Should I then explain it with a reason confused through great suffering?

To fathom such a mystery, I would have to think logically. "Logic" comes from *logos*. To be pleasant to Christ, the *Logos*, you must think and act logically. In the original Greek we are asked in Romans 12:1 to bring to the Lord "a logical sacrifice". Clarity and accuracy in thought are expected of Christ's disciples. But for a long time I have lacked these qualities. Hunger, the remembrance of tortures, the fear of new ones as often as the cell is unlocked, the whole atmosphere of solitary confinement in a subterranean cell, all combine to make logical thinking impossible. Perhaps there are also drugs in my scanty food. I cannot tell you what it is exactly with the Jews.

You cannot become a Jew by practising the Jewish religion, just as you cannot become a lion by roaring or devouring raw flesh. I am sure that birth cannot make you a Jew any more than being born in a garage can make you an automobile. To be a Jew is more than belonging to a nation. It is a calling which you do not get by natural birth. Born a Jew, you must realise your calling.

What makes the Jew – the man who is essentially Jewish and really deserves this high appellation, the man who is loyal to the King of the Jews – dangerous for the world and difficult to bear even for the children of God from among the Gentiles, is that the Jewish Christian is a restless fighter.

He has learned from Abraham's experience. Abraham met Melchizedek only after his return from a slaughter in which he had bathed his sword in blood (Genesis 14:17). He had not met him during prayer, nor when he brought sacrifices. He met him after a fight.

Battlefields are our tabernacles. Captains of hosts are

our priests. Our liturgy is a clashing of swords. Our incense is the smoke of burning Sodoms. Jews and Christians have burned on stakes long enough. Our priestly cassocks are armour. Thus clothed we enter Jehu's chariot. We are Jonadabs, his fellow-warriors. Our icons are living soldiers to whom we pay our homage. Our God is a consuming fire.

This is the religion about which I am passionate. This is how I feel my role as a Jewish Christian. If there is no place for me in such a tabernacle, I would like to live at least in its shadow, but the churches of the Gentiles are too well-ordered, calm, settled, boring for me.

A Jewish Christian loves his nation as Esther did. Therefore Pharaohs and Hamans, as well as cowards among the believers, tremble at our approach.

So many genial Jews have missed the mark in serving foreign masters. Joseph served Egypt, Daniel Babylon, Marx the world proletariat, Disraeli the British empire, Léon Blum social democracy and France. Some of these were children of God, others the opposite, but in either case their earthly benefactors soon forgot their services. Those who embody what is essential in the appellation Hebrew-Christian would never serve any other cause than that of the people of God.

In their relationship with God, they are not satisfied with forgiveness of sins. They want their lives changed.

Our responsibility is entirely different from that of other believers. St. Paul writes "Unto them [the Jews] were committed the oracles of God." Every line in the Bible was written by a Jew. That St. Luke might have been a Greek is an invention. If he were not a Jew he could not have been a Biblical author. This thought outdoes all guesses about his origin. Luther contested the authority of the ecumenical councils because they were not constituted of Jews. Once they were composed of Gentiles, their decisions could not be considered the oracles of God, compulsory for Christians. Jewish Christians are called to evoke the truth as it was in its nakedness, before being clothed in parables.

Today many parables have become obsolete.

Outside, farming has been collectivised. No man possesses a hundred sheep any more. Who cares if one is lost? It is state property. Fathers don't have inheritances to impart to profligate sons. When they get into trouble, there is nobody who possesses swine who might hire them. They have to be state employees, and they would not be free to leave their job to return to the father. Kings cannot arrange marriage feasts for their sons any more. They have been dethroned. Beggars can no longer hope for alms at the door of rich men. The capitalists have been expropriated, deported to some slave labour camps. They would be willing to beg for a piece of bread themselves, but for a situation epitomised in a little joke:

What is the difference between a pessimist and an optimist? The optimist says, "With this regime, we will all become beggars," to which the pessimist replies, "But from whom will we beg?"

Jesus' parables presented eternal truth clad in episodes taken from social life, which has changed completely. The Hebrew-Christian divests truth of its temporary clothing and sees it as it is.

The real Hebrew-Christian does not remain satisfied with what he is told about Jesus, even by the saintliest of teachers. St. Luke writes in his Gospel (1:2) about some who had been eyewitnesses of the events. Who had been an eyewitness of Mary's virgin birth, of the pre-existence of Jesus, of His solitary nights of prayer? The Greek does not have the word "eyewitness" but *autoptes*, a word composed of *auto* (self) and *optes* (those who have seen).

Luke speaks about men who have seen things themselves or (1:3) who "have had perfect understanding of all things *anothen*", which means literally "being looked upon from above".

There are men who are seated in heavenly places, outside of time and space. They see what is happening in heaven and look down upon what has happened and is happening on earth. They also see things which normally remain hidden. Luke was such a man; so were the other Evangelists. Do you really believe that there are no more seers in Israel?

They see, and when given even by Jesus the choice of having Himself or the Holy Spirit, the Comforter, who does not come unless Jesus departs from us (John 16:7), they do not fall into the trap: they do not ask for more fullness and more gifts of the Spirit. For them the Spirit is no Comforter. There can be no comfort for the absence of Jesus.

Rachel, when her children were slain, wept for them and would not be comforted (Matt. 2:18). What unnatural mother a woman must be to accept comfort when what she needs is her child returned to her.

The Hebrew Christian has all due respect for the Spirit but desires Jesus. Without Him, honey tastes like gall. The Spirit is a spirit of truth which testifies about Jesus. But they do not desire even a true testimony about an absent Jesus, not even one of divine origin. They wish Jesus Himself.

Having the Spirit, we could rightly solve many problems. But we do not wish to solve problems. Mary Magdalene did not seek solutions. Rather, she sat quietly at His feet. Time somehow solves problems without our intervention. We just wish to see His sunny face and hear His melodious voice.

The real Hebrew Christian is a man apart, even

within the church. The time when people will take hold of his skirt in order to be taught the Word of God may be far away, but he will never compromise, he will never lower the standard in order to win popularity.

Tomorrow I might be confronted with something entirely different: "Take off your shirt in order to be beaten with a whip." I will comply. A paper containing a statement that I renounce my faith and denounce my brethren could free me. What really separates me from my beloved ones, then, is a paper wall, not these heavy quarries which I see. So for many centuries a book has separated the Jews from other peoples.

I will remain, by the grace of God, on this side of the paper wall. But I am thankful for the high calling of being a Jewish Christian, and I will not capitulate. Amen.

# THE BELOVED COMMUNISTS

BELOVED FLOCK OF CHRIST

I would poison myself if I thought of Communists only with malice.

Once while beating me the captain amused himself by singing tango music. I would have been simply unfair to writhe under the beating without appreciating the other aspect of reality. He had a beautiful voice and the tune was pleasant to the ear. If I resented the beating, I had to be thankful for the music. It is a rare treat for a prisoner to hear somebody singing beautifully.

If only we could always appreciate the dual aspects of reality, the fact that it takes both sides to make a whole! When I feel a pain, there is always the joy of being a living "I" who feels. The "I" may feel pain now, but these same nerves are capable of feeling caresses too. It is admirable to have sensitive nerves. It is wise to appreciate the joy of possessing them even while suffering pain.

The Jews are a chosen people. It is also a chosen thing to have a Jew as a torturer. He accompanies his wickedness with such splendid jokes. At a certain moment, when I could bear no more, I cried, "Leave me, leave me!" I had difficulty breathing.

My torturers consulted with each other. The Jew among them told a joke: "Two men entered a tram. One held onto the strap. The second was small and kept his stability by holding onto the beard of another man. The man protested. 'Let go of my beard!' The Jew asked, 'Why should I? Are you getting off at the next station?' Why should we leave Wurmbrand alone? Will he die?''

I hear their songs, their jokes. I enjoy them. I owe them gratitude.

But most of all, I owe them pity.

The Communists have never pondered Shakespeare's words, "Uneasy lies the head that wears the crown." They took the crown from legitimate authority, King Michael. They hoped to become happier through this. They have only become busier. Now they have to scheme day and night how to maintain and consolidate their positions.

Actually, I have it better than they. Discharged of all responsibilities, I can lie quietly in my cell and be happy as much as I decide to. For a time, I disturbed my own happiness by spying on myself and tore myself to pieces for every false thought. But to spy upon yourself is as wrong and impolite as spying upon someone else. I have given it up.

Now I listen attentively when Communists speak to me during my interrogation sessions. I am learning an art which I should have learned long ago, the art of allowing the adversary to say everything on his heart, even when he is wrong.

Once back in my cell, I make the Communists the subject of my meditation and prayer. I also think about the many others around me who are oppressed by the Communists because they believe in God. I think about what this does to God.

In the Hebrew original it is written, "The Lord's soul was shortened for the misery of Israel" (Judges 10:16). A God whose children are persecuted is an amputated God. Look at North Africa, which was originally one of the foremost centres of Christianity. The Moslems conquered the provinces, and for centuries millions have passed through this earthly life without coming to a knowledge of salvation. Could He not bring the Gospel to them without the church? He could not.

He is a handicapped God and needs help like any other amputee. Deborah sang, "Curse ye Meroz, said the angel of the Lord, curse ye bitterly the inhabitants thereof; because *they came not to the help of the Lord.*" And as if these words were not enough, the angel repeated, "*to the help of the Lord against the mighty*" (Judges 5:23).

The Lord needs help. Yes, He *needs* help. He will never succeed without our help. And we sit in chains. How can I decide to be happy, knowing this? If this is the situation, I have to be concerned. I have to give up what I had decided a few minutes before, that is, to whistle joyfully and to dance around in my cell.

My minds gets confused again. How do I know? Because again I made the mistake of spying on myself to find out how my mind is. I'll leave it as it is, and I will think about the Communists whom I love.

Long ago the Lord had predicted "upon the earth distress of nations, with perplexity:... Men's hearts failing them for fear, and for looking after those things which are coming on the earth" (Luke 21:25, 26).

These words have had a multiple fulfilment: at the destruction of the Jewish state in AD 71, at the close of the sixth century when hordes of heathen warriors swept down upon what was left of the decaying civilisation of the Roman Empire, during the Moslem invasion, and at the end of the eighteenth century in the French Revolution. Now it happens again.

The actual catastrophes could have been averted. Unsolved social questions have brought upon us the great crises of our day. One could very well deduce that the Christian's response should be activism, militant participation in the struggle against evil. Popes, Orthodox priests, and Protestants have warned against what might happen if Christians defaulted.

Arnold Toynbee once told a meeting of working men, "We Christians have neglected you. Instead of justice, we have offered you hard and unreal advice. But I think we are changing. If you would only believe it and trust us! There are many of us who would spend our lives in your service." The audience jeered and yelled, "Nobody wants you to." Toynbee was stung to the heart, went home, and died.

The Orthodox priest Gapon had been the first to organise a demonstration of St. Petersburg's proletariat. With ikons in their hands they marched towards the palace of the Czar to assure him of their loyalty and to ask for the improvement of their life. The police shot at the demonstrators. Then the Communists took over the movement. They hanged the Orthodox priest.

The church has lost the opportunity to win the proletariat to its side. We have given them into the hands of the Communists, because we preferred a comfortable life. We were not ready to fight in order to win souls.

The story is old. When Gideon told an army of 32,000 Jewish warriors, "Whosoever is fearful and afraid, let him return and depart," two-thirds of the army took advantage of the proposal (Judges 7:3). We want to be Christians without being involved in battle.

But it is written about Jesus that He will lead captivity captive, which means that His love will captivate those who are now Satan's captives.

I don't know how. The Vulgate adds to the Hebrew of Judges 5:8: "The Lord chose a new species of war and Himself subverted the gates of the enemy. Ten thousand men, scarcely armed and led by a woman, defeated a strong and well-equipped army." When the Lord willed, He sent an angel to take a peasant, Gideon, from the threshing floor and make him a general. Many centuries later, a peasant girl, St. Joan of Arc, who had never ridden a horse nor held a sword in her hand, led the French army to victory. God chooses the most unlikely instruments.

Dear brothers and sisters, He might have chosen the most unqualified of you to bring to Christ a multitude of Communists. We must be as intent on attaining our purposes as they are on attaining theirs.

In the free world, it is customary during a strike for men to picket the entrance to a factory. They often use violence to keep from entering workers who choose not to join their actions. Likewise we Christians must decide to boycott hell, picketing the entrance with determination.

When I was a boy of fourteen, a friend took me for the first time into a bordello. I was so ashamed and frightened that I fled. But why were there no priests, pastors, or Christian laymen picketing the entrance to such houses of perdition, stopping every teenager and telling him the risks he will incur to his soul?

We must learn to picket. We must surround hell with a cordon and simply not allow the Communists to enter in. If they insist, they can enter the abyss only by stepping over our dead bodies. Our opposition should be that strong.

God will not abolish hell if we think like this. If He had none, His laws would not be authoritative. But perhaps it will remain empty.

Following His dire predictions for our day, Jesus added, "When these things begin to come to pass, look up, and lift up your heads; for *your* redemption draws nigh" (Luke 21:28). From these words one might conclude that the Christian is to shun activism and lead a contemplative life. Therefore, don't try to stop the onward rush of events; don't look around wondering whom you might save. Whatever these dreadful events may bring to others, to *you* they bring eternal salvation. Keep this joyful expectation in the midst of calamity. "Behold the fig tree, and all the trees; when they now shoot forth, ye see and know of your own selves that summer is now nigh at hand" (Luke 21:29, 30).

The Lord compares these awe-inspiring events, these political and social cataclysms, with the budding of soft green leaves in spring. You can enjoy them and lead a quiet life. It is not up to you to change God's decree if He has decided to punish this world.

I cannot take this attitude recommended only to some. There are different characters, different callings. Some are called to battle, some to still waters. I could not tell you which of these two ways is more legitimate. But for myself, I cannot help choosing the first.

# VISITING MYSELF

DEAR BRETHREN AND SISTERS

As a pastor I used to make daily house calls. I was much impressed by a story told by Bishop Latimer to his clergy during the Reformation:

> It would be too much to ask you to be pastors such as Jesus was. I would propose another model of a good pastor: Lucifer. He visits his whole parish daily, every house, rich and poor. And when he enters a house, he does not speak only to the adults. He has a story or fairy tale prepared for every child, suitable for just his age. Before leaving, he also enters the kitchen and says something nice to the maid. Learn from him how to perform your pastoral duties.

So preaching and writing books or articles were not my principal tasks. A pastor is not a maker of sermons but a maker of saints. Only the people I visited know how frequently I have been in their homes.

Brother X is now in the same row of cells with me. He recently reminded me on our "wireless" how he had backslidden at one time.

When I rang the bell at his house (it was on a cold winter's day), he opened the door and told me, "I won't receive you any more. I don't want to have anything to do with pastors." With this he slammed the door.

# Visiting Myself

I shouted loudly, "Well, I'll wait outside until you change your mind." So I waited, standing in the snow. He observed me from behind the window curtain. After a time he came out to the gate and shouted,

"Go away! I won't receive you. You'll catch pneumonia."

"What I have to tell you is very important," I replied. "It is worth the risk. I can wait."

In the end, he allowed me in and gave me a cup of hot tea. Now he is probably happy to be on the way of the cross.

As a pastor I also visited with God several times a day. A Christian can have fellowship with Him. With boldness he can "enter into the holiest by the blood of Jesus" (Heb. 10:19).

God also has a habit of visiting people. He walked and talked with the first couple in the Garden of Eden. He visisted Abraham and Jacob, Moses and Joshua.

Though I had visited with men and God, there was one person in my parish whom I had neglected completely. I had never visited myself. It is written about the prodigal son that "he came to himself." How rarely this happens! Men travel the world over to visit other cultures and meet new people but never knock at the gate of their own person and say, "Good morning, dear sir Myself. I have come to talk to you a little while." For the prodigal son, coming to himself meant a return to true thinking. One visit with himself was enough to send him back to his father. How many times I had read this story without coming to this conclusion.

Richard III had visited himself before the fatal battle of Bosworth. He discovered much of himself (in words given to him by Shakespeare):

Is there a murderer here? No. Yes, I am:

Then fly. What? From myself? Great reason: why?
Lest I revenge. What? myself upon myself?
Alack! I love myself. Wherefore? For any good
That I myself have done unto myself?
O no: alas! I rather hate myself
For hateful deeds committed by myself.
I am a villain. Yet I lie; I am not.
Fool, of thyself speak well. Fool, do not flatter.
My conscience hath a thousand several tongues,
And every tongue brings in a several tale,
And every tale condemns me for a villain.

And so, like the prodigal son and Richard III, I decide to visit myself.

"Hello, Me, how are you doing? I wish to have a chat with you. We don't speak the same language. In my language I tell you I wish to speak with you. You would interpret it as me wishing to speak with me. But let us not lose ourselves in semantics. Here am I and here are you, the 'me'. Let us visit for a while."

"What would you like to know from me?"

"First of all, what is your real name? In Hebrew your name is Reuben; in Romanian, Richard. You have written under the pseudonym Radu Valentin. The jailors changed your name to Vasile Georgescu. You have had so many nicknames. And then this common name 'Richard' sounds so different when pronounced by different persons. Since you were thrown in this cell, you have heard a voice giving you a new name. After a long time the same voice gave you another name. You are more distinguished than the conquerors in the book of Revelation, who are promised *one* new name (Rev. 2:17). You are far from being a conqueror, and heaven has already given you two."

"Don't be so harsh. Araunah (II. Sam. 24) is called in

80

God's Word by several names. Also, one and the same king is called Uzziah and Azariah in II Kings 15, and he is called Ozias in Matthew 1. God Himself has many names. But as to your main question, I cannot answer it. Once I told the Lord in prayer that since I was alone, without Bible or other religious books, without sermons, without brethren, He should speak to me directly. If He could speak to Pharaoh and Nebuchadnezzar, He could speak to me, too, even if I were the last of evildoers. Then I heard His voice (His sheep normally hear it) asking me the same question you ask: 'What is your name?' Now that you mention it, I wonder if I was wrong in attributing the voice to the Lord. Perhaps it was just you. I do not seem to realise yet how split I am. I might interpret as external voices, as revelations from God or whispers from the devil, what are just internal dialogues of a personality divided in two."

"What did you answer the Lord?"

"Stop being hypocritical! You know the answer to that. I can't be fooled any more. It was you who put the question, and it was 'me' who gave the answer. But as you wish to play this game, I'll tell you the story. I did not know the answer. I can introduce myself to everybody as Richard. But how do I tell Jesus that my name is Richard? Am I worthy of this name?

"St..Richard was an English peasant who, in a time of fierce persecution, was ordered to be imprisoned for his faith. When the arresting constable mounted his horse to ride to him, the animal went berserk, throwing his rider and injuring him fatally. So now Richard was charged with murder. The prosecution had a clear case. If he had not been a believer, the constable would not have mounted the horse to pick him up and so would not have fallen and died. As you see, Communist justice has had its predecessors.

"And now Richard was on the gallows. The hangman had difficulty fixing the noose of the rope. Richard, who was so good he could not bear to trouble anyone, bowed to the executioner and asked, 'May I help you? I am a peasant skilled in these things.' Allowed to do so, he fixed the noose, thanked the hangman graciously for his kind permission, and passed away. For this loving attitude toward the executioner and for his gentleness in all things he was given the name St. Richard. How could I dare to tell Jesus that I bear the same name as this man?

"Should I tell Him that I am a Christian? With the proud words *Christianus sum*, 'I am a Christian,' the first disciples fearlessly entered the arena to be devoured by lions. I have often stood before a cage of lions at the zoo and asked myself honestly, 'Could I do that?' My answer is always, 'No, I would rather recant.'

"Well, to finish my story, I bowed to Jesus and told Him, 'Lord, I have no name. Allow me to take Yours and to say like Paul that it is not I who live, but You in me.' So He allowed it. At least, that is what I thought at the time. Now I know that it was all a mistake. You allowed it; that is, I gave myself the kind permission to be called by the name of Christ. I am unsurpassed in humility, it seems."

"Keep to the rules of the game. We are two different persons. I am I and you are you. If you say that you are no longer you, but that Christ lives in you, let us draw the ultimate conclusion. Perhaps you have no individual soul any more. Buddhists deny its existence. Salvation consists in being freed from the illusion of having a soul. Would you agree now? Ha, ha. I caught you there. If you answer, you live still. And if you don't answer, I have triumphed in this discussion. I could do this only because I am. And as you and I are one and the same person, we continued to live – unlike Paul, who asserted that he had ceased to be."

"I have nothing to answer. I cannot tell you in words anything about myself, not even whether I exist. A man described in words is not the real man, any more than a God described in words is the real God. It is useless to continue along these lines."

"Then may I ask you another question? Do you have the Holy Spirit?"

"I surely have Him, but He does not have me. The union is an unhappy one. But you are comical. You are a prisoner. So am I. And here we sit discussing metaphysics when my mind is obsessed with just one thought: I am terribly hungry. I would eat acorns, grass, mice – anything. My wife must also be in some cell. Her predominant obsession must also be hunger."

His talking about hunger reminded me of my stomach. The visit ceased without even a polite word of parting. I simply was alone again. As usual, the physiological was victorious. I am hungry, and I am indignant against the churches of the West, about whose riches I have heard, some of which spend on chandeliers what could feed us all for a whole month. And I am angry with those who keep us hungry. Love, like every other spiritual energy, is food transformed and sublimated. When you are very hungry, how can you love the one who starves you?

I am sorry I could not finish the discussion I had when I visisted myself. I would have liked to ask myself just one more question: "Do you approve of violence against atheist tyrants?"

You have eaten. Visit God, visit your brethren, but never forget to visit yourself too. The prodigal son "came to himself". Amen.

# NEW YEAR

HAPPY NEW YEAR, MY BELOVED FRIENDS

Outside, the wardens interrupt the silence. They wish one another a happy new year. It is midnight. The year 1948 has passed. I cannot congratulate Jesus. It has been 1915 years since He was crucified. The 1916th nail will now be driven into His cross.

I know that every doubt of mine causes Him more pain, as if a new dart were piercing His heart. But He has asked us to go further than that, if necessary, in order to have life. He invites us to eat His flesh and drink His blood, as lions devour an innocent victim, as if it were only by disembowelling the Godhead that we can find out what it is. He wishes to be known more than He wishes to be caressed. Excessive desire to know the truth is not a vice. I cannot live without knowing God. I don't consider modesty in questioning Him a virtue.

There was a time when Jesus "had no fault, or I no fault could spy, when He was all beauty or all blindness I".

But now, since I have nothing left in this whole world but my wit to live by, it has begun to value itself very highly. All else seems of little importance. My wit has questions to ask and I cannot stop it.

I have liked very much the story of St. Christopher. He was branded with red-hot irons, roasted over a fire, and cooked in boiling oil, but suffered no pain and was

84

not bothered by this kind of treatment. Observing this, almost fifty thousand persons were converted. A drop of the saint's blood healed someone who was accidentally injured while watching Christopher's execution.

I like a God who does miracles of such magnitude.

I realise now that the New Testament had never satisfied me really, because I found the miracles recounted there much too small for the Son of God. Three people were resurrected, but millions of corpses remained dead. Only three families had the comfort of seeing their beloved ones restored to life. Many widows whose only sons died remained without consolation. Jesus stilled a storm, but on so small a lake as Galilee. Tempests on the ocean sank countless ships, and men drowned. He did not help them. On one occasion 4,000 and on another 5,000 (plus women and children) had a good dinner through miracles performed by Him. What about the next day when they were hungry again? And what about the millions who have starved throughout the ensuing centuries?

He sent an angel to free Peter from prison. The incident stands alone. James was beheaded, and since then thousands have been martyred. Why?

How can the world go on? It is New Year's Eve. Everywhere people speak to each other, trying to spread joy among themselves.

Solomon sacrificed in Gibeon, a place forbidden by law because the tabernacle was not there (I Kings 3:4). You did not mind but spoke words of goodness and blessing in that place to the man who, even after he had a vision of You, continued to do many wicked things. I might be wicked, too, but have pity on a lonely man. I know You do only small miracles. Do just a very little thing more. Speak to one single prisoner out of thousands.

I don't understand You. Don't You have power enough? Don't You have the will to wipe away *all* tears? Could You make only a couple of big saints like Christopher? Why did he not suffer pain when he was burned? Why did St. Lawrence engage in pleasantries while roasted on a gridiron, whereas I feel intensely even the pain of a slap or a kick? Over 45,000 were converted at Christopher's death. Even this does not satisfy me, as I always decried the boasting of evangelists about how many decided for Christ at their meetings. I compared their figures with those who had decided on the same night for pubs, gambling houses, places of perdition, and heathen religions.

Love is compared with death in Song of Solomon 8:6. Death is satisfied with nothing less than absolutely all men. Till now only two have escaped death: Enoch and Elijah. But some say they will come back to earth and will be the prophets that are slain, about whom we are told in Revelation 11. If so, they will have to pay their tribute to death, too.

As death wants everyone, so I want all men for the Kingdom.

I made a crucifix out of bread, an ugly crucifix. I had never modelled anything before. And the bread was darker than most bread.

I look to You hanging on the cross. You are silent. Again I have to guess what Your answer may be.

If I were in the puplit today dressed in a beautiful cassock, I would speak about the one great miracle, that a lonely Galilean who hung upon a horrible cross became the subject of thousands of confident songs, that the painful execution of a Man deemed a criminal proved to be the means of salvation for the whole world.

But inwardly I would be dissatisfied. What you have

done is beautiful, but too little for an almighty God who could make the whole drama cease at once. Why are You silent?

Perhaps it is not good for me to know or to escape suffering. Perhaps suffering is the way to the other shore. But are You not almighty? Could you not have made an easier way, so that men might get to heaven by passing through valleys in which roses and lilies grow?

Probably *I* am too small – not Your miracles. I am a disciple of Yours. But Christianity is the only profession in the world in which men remain disciples for life and never become independent workers. As for the few workers, they don't strive to become master builders (I Cor. 3:10), as were Paul, Peter, Thomas, Catherine of Siena, Calvin, and Luther. How could an architect explain his designs to a disciple? Only a master builder could understand him.

If I grow, I will know. You are like Gulliver among dwarfs. Even You cannot bow so low that we may be able to understand something. We have to take the word of Augustine: "Whatever right reason suggests to you as more perfect, you may be sure that God has already made it, for He is the creator of all things good." I suppose that all the beautiful things I crave exist, but I cannot see them yet.

We must also reject the mistaken notion that a whole can be perfect only if each of its parts is perfect.

Iago is vicious, an intrigue-maker and a liar, but he is a necessary part in a perfect work of art, *Othello*. For my part, I am in a small cell. We are all confined to too small a world. Imperfections seen by me can be a useful part of a perfect reality.

Thank You for one more year. I will try to use it well for growth. Perhaps I will question You less next New Year's Eve.

# BEFORE SUICIDE

DEAR BRETHREN AND SISTERS

After producing many beautiful compositions, Robert Schumann began to hear bizarre noises in his head. He spoke about "a splendid music, played by instruments which give more beautiful tunes than those existing on earth". He tried to write them down. The result was cacophony. But he desired only that music. One day he threw himself into the Rhine. Fishermen saved him, but his mind was gone. He died in an asylum.

Suicide or madness will probably be my end too, because I have also heard strange music. I can't even try to notate it, not being skilled at composing music, so I will try to explain it in words. Pray while listening. But be careful it is music that invites you to leave this world.

A Russian brother related to us how he once explained the Gospel to a young girl. He told her about the Paradise that awaits the believer. She put her trust in Jesus. One stormy winter day she left the house. The next morning she was found frozen to death, with bared breast. Did she undress herself in order to die and go more quickly to Paradise? We shall never know. But strange things happen in mysterious, holy Russia. We had given Bibles to Russian soldiers. Later, one of them entered a church and slaughtered a lamb before the image of Jesus. This was the little he had understood from the Bible, and he acted upon it without hesitancy.

The music I hear is an invitation not to wait for a paradise after death but to come to it immediately. If you want to see this music in an image, look at a statue of Krishna dancing and playing a flute to invite girls to come to his temple. But don't think you have seen an idol. Rather, it is an archetype of the collective unconscious. It is music that invites you to do the most foolish and unacceptable things because that is how it impresses you. The explanation for what you felt you had to do comes later. It was the music that caused the Jews to say at Mount Sinai, "*Naase venishma*" – "We will do and we will hear" (Ex. 24:7). The doing comes before the hearing – not the contrary.

But there is also something else in this music, something terrifying, that drives you mad.

For a long time I have made it a habit to be awake only during the night. Great spiritual battles are usually fought at night. You sense in the darkness the occult forces that inspire murderers and thieves, who also perform their works of iniquity during the night. Stalin worked during the whole night.

I pray for a time and then just listen. From immeasurable Satanic depths, fiery darts are thrown at the soul. St. Marguerite Alacoque once saw the virgin Mary, who told her, "I wish to put in your heart a few of the darts which hurt me and my Son." The devil also wishes to make you share his pain. Once his dart enters your heart, even manna becomes tasteless to you. You prefer to remain hungry rather than eat something that comes from God.

During the war a badly wounded SS officer fell prisoner to the British. He urgently needed a blood transfusion. He asked, "What kind of blood will it be?" He was told, "British." His reply was, "I prefer to die rather than have non-German blood introduced into my veins." He stuck to his convictions till death overtook him.

This tune is the counterpoint to God's music. You can never hear the latter without Satan's accompaniment to it, which is even more attractive to our hearts than the angelic choir.

"Commit suicide," this music commands. "You are called to be great. Why do you need Jesus as your Messiah? What if you are the Messiah? Or, if you consider the place of the Messiah already occupied, the role of Antichrist is still free. He will rule the world. People once described you as a fascinating preacher. Thus your fascination could be increased. Just try." And then you hear serene, calm, angelic playing on harps. It is so beautiful you remain in ecstasies before it, but it does not convince. It does not satisfy desire like the first.

Once I had the experience of speaking with a messenger of a Satanist conventicle. I had never seen him before. Even now I could not explain how it happened that one day I found myself sitting before him. What he told me and what he proposed to me was so terrible that I never told it to anyone except saintly Bishop Muller, who I knew would take the secret to his grave. Does this conventicle have the means of pursuing me by telepathy even in my subterranean cell? But it is those with a persecution complex who feel themselves pursued by inimical forces. So perhaps I am already a madman. On the other hand, I cannot see how one can be as badly persecuted as I am without being paranoid.

How about my beginning to persecute them? If they can influence men to evil from afar, I could pursue them with good on condition that I become a great centre of spiritual energy. Here you have megalomania following the mania of persecution. Where can I find the answers?

With God? Then isn't it best to commit suicide and go ask Him directly, since here on earth He leaves my mind blurred?

Here or in some other world I want to spread good far away. To love my neighbour is too little for me. Jesus promised that the righteous will shine like suns in the kingdom of the Father. A sun gives life to billions of beings. He has promised this, and I will not accept less. I have become righteous through faith in Jesus. He did not say that the righteous will have to wait decades until they die and then become suns. I have to become a sun immediately, to fill the world with light and goodness, to bring whole nations to Christ.

Theologians would tell me that it is not my responsibility to do this, but it must be done by the church universal, of which I am only a small part. But theology ceases at the threshold of this prison and on the threshold of madness.

I wish to be a Christ in miniature. The words "a miniature" are a concession on my part. This call, too, is in the music I hear. I cannot put it in words, even as Schumann could not put it into notes. He went mad and threw himself into the river. After hearing this music, you tell Jesus, "Give Yourself to me wholly, or leave me wholly." Amen.

# MY GREATNESS

DEAR BRETHREN AND SISTERS

Preachers in the pulpit should be very careful about what they say and how they say it. They must be selective. I must not. Why? King Abimelech and Phichol, the chief captain of his host, said to Abraham, "God is with thee in *all* that thou doest" (Genesis 21:22). I can say all I think. I am blessed in everything.

A fly once sat quietly on the horn of a bull. After a while, overcome by scruples, it said, "Mr. Bull, it may be that my presence here displeases you. If so, I apologise and will leave."

"Don't feel bad," the bull answered. "You can bring your whole family to live on my horn. It really does not matter to me."

Peter was called a rock (Matt. 16:18). It is a matter of indifference to a rock from which side the wind blows.

I have become hard like a horn. Therefore, come, thoughts of whatever kind; better plague me instead of plaguing someone else. I can bear you.

I can even bear the proud feeling that I am important. Not only can I bear it, I have to evoke it, because pride is an essential part of megalomania. I have decided to be mad. I have not yet chosen my specific kind of madness. But I incline towards this.

There are two extremes. King Lear prayed, "O, let me not be mad, not mad, sweet heaven. Keep me in

93

temper, I would not be mad." His prayer was not answered. He became mad. Rimbaud, on the contrary, had made it his aim to practise a long, tremendous, and reasoned derangement of all his senses in order to reach the unknown. If reason proved itself unable to reach the unknown, he concluded, how else could it be reached than through disordering reason intentionally? He never became mad, though he did become very vicious.

Jesus, St. Paul, and the apostles must have worked upon their characters in a certain way in order to convince so many men that they were mad or drunk.

The Beghards in the thirteenth century must have done something, similar to what some Pentecostals do nowadays, to help spread the rumour about them that they made wolfish howlings in their fits of religious raving.

In a sense, everybody is mad. Some are mad for money, others for sexual partners. The Communists are mad for power. I wish definitely to be mad for God. Just as one has to work oneself up to the other kinds of madness, one has to work oneself up for this, too. It seems that it is human destiny to become mad. If it is our fate to be drowned, then rather in a sea of perfume than in a ditch of mud.

There exists also a mad loyalty. One of Shakespeare's fools said:

> That, sir, which serves and seeks for gain
> And follows but for form,
> Will pack when it begins to rain
> And leave thee in the storm.
> But I will tarry, the fool will stay
> And let the wise man fly.

If I remain reasonable, there is a good chance that I will

end by betraying the underground Church. Only fools can remain loyal when they are so terribly hungry.

I am quite determined to become mad. My madness will be to believe that I have the Godhead living in me. Whoever thinks like this is called by others a megalomaniac. And the accusation is not even false. Such a man really considers himself great.

The commandments on Moses' tablets are given in the singular form. Not "ye" but "thou" shalt not do this or that. God tells *me* how to behave. Christ says, "Blessed art *thou*" (Matt. 16:17) to the man to whom it is revealed that Jesus is the Son of God. *My* defects are criticised in the Bible. So I must be imporant. The Bible is God's dialogue with *me*.

The renowned Jewish philosopher Spinoza once wrote, "There is no foe to progress like self-conceit and the laziness which self-conceit begets." But prison life is not favourable to the development of humility.

Just because we are continually abused, dressed in what looks like zebra-skins, beaten, insulted daily with obscene words, an over-compensation takes place in our minds. I must be very important if such a powerful movement as Communism, which rules unchallenged one third of the world, considers it absolutely necessary to keep me in an isolated, subterranean cell and endeavours to break my body and mind. If they did not do so, my life in liberty could endanger their existence.

I am unspeakably hungry. I think sometimes about those who survived the Nobile expedition to the North Pole and were suspected of having eaten the corpse of one of their comrades who had frozen to death. I wonder if I would not have done the same thing.

There is mould on my bread. It is green. As often as I get it – once a week – it reminds me of Psalm 23: "He makes me to lie down in *green* pastures." My whole body has tremblings which I cannot control.

I cannot speak well any more. I have not spoken for years. I stutter when I report in a few words a need to a warden. One of them told me, "You're an idiot. Don't you see that you can't even formulate a sentence?" He said this to one who remembered being considered a good preacher in times past.

I could easily yield to the strong impulse to become a madman in the full sense of the word, if I did not know that I am surrounded by the love of a multitude of Christians, by a real wall of prayers, as many other Christians are not. What makes me so important in their eyes?

What in my preaching and in myself is so great that the Communists have to warn men against my influence and seek to break me?

Am I really great?

I believe I am. I vaguely remember the name of Bernhard de Palissy as the inventor of porcelain. He was a Protestant, and the French King Henry III, a Catholic, to whom he had endeared himself, said to him one day, "I will be compelled to give you up to your enemies unless you change your religion."

Palissy answered, "I pity you for having given utterance to the words 'I shall be compelled.' What unkingly words! No power in the world can compel me, a manufacturer of earthenware, to change my convictions because a mob wills it."

All my torturers are compelled to torture me. They know that if they refuse they will share my fate. I am beyond compulsion. So are all my brethren in faith. Therefore we are the only ones who really exist. I *am*, because I am myself. And I am great, because I am *I*.

There is a hymn "How Great *Thou* Art." In the maddening circumstances of the solitary cell, I could almost compose a hymn, "How Great *I* Am," I, the Bible's only concern.

The Bible tells me about *my* salvation, about God's being amazingly eager to have *me* in His Heaven.

Scripture does not solve national problems. A scrap of newspaper found in the toilet informed us that the state of Israel was founded. Judaism will not have solved its worries through this event. The new state will have its trouble, just as Romanians who were never scattered have had theirs, going from one distress to another. Empires have passed away without ever having their problems solved.

The Bible does not solve the problem of the division of mankind into social classes. "The poor always ye have with you" (John 12:8).

The Bible does not solve religious problems. Two thousand years after Christ there are still hundreds of religions. Christianity itself is divided.

The Bible speaks about me.

I must be important if my captors strive so hard to break me and God strives so hard to uplift me.

The Bible speaks about me as being a god (John 10:34), a sinner (Rom. 3:23), a seed (1 Cor. 15:42), and the ground (Matt. 13:8). The Kingdom of God is within me (Luke 17:21). Would you like to know where Christ lives? I can give you His exact address: "Christ lives in me" (Gal. 2:20), within *me*, the abused prisoner kept in prison cell No. 7. I am dust (Gen. 3:19), but a dust apart, which will live eternally (John 11:25).

If a man renounces everything for Christ's sake, everything becomes full of Him. How can one be humble when he fills the universe? How can one be humble when he can speak the seemingly blasphemous words which put him on an equal footing with God, "I can do all things" (Phil. 4:13)? Let the addition be "through Christ who strengthens me." Whatever the circumstances that make me so powerful, it still remains that I am great. "I can do all things."

In modern languages "God of Abraham" or "God of Isaac" are three words. In Hebrew the corresponding expression *Elohei-Abraham*, united by the orthographical sign called *mappekh*, makes "God of Abraham" a single word. God can leave me only if He takes me with Him, so united have we become. The Kabala says, "God with Israel is God. God without Israel is not God."

I pace up and down my small cell. It has room for three steps. I do not allow my captors to dictate how many steps I should walk; I always walk just two steps. This limited space I occupy falsely tempts me to consider myself small and insignificant. We all live in too-small inner universes. We are great. When Jesus arranged the miraculous draught of fish, He allowed only *great* fish to enter the net (John 21:11).

We are one with God through Christ. God is one. He is so much one that in giving birth to a Son, in emanating the Spirit, in uniting with millions of men, He never abandons His absolute oneness. Schiller complained, "Two souls live within my breast." He should have thrown them both out and allowed himself the privilege of an indestructible oneness with God. Then he would have been great without ever having written a poem or drama. There would be no need of a pedestal any more in order to seem great.

I sit hungry, with chains on my legs, in a subterranean cell. I stutter when I speak some banality and I am great.

As children of God we are so great that we do not have to fear the supernatural world. It fears us. St. James wrote, "Resist the devil, and he will flee from you." The devil did not flee from the archangel Michael but battled courageously against him (Rev. 12:7). From me he simply flees. The disciples of the Lord can drive out demons with a few simple words.

The Indian Christian mystic Sadhu Sundar Singh once found himself in the Himalayas and entered a cave to rest. But as soon as he lay down, he observed in the depths of the cave the glimmering eyes of a tiger. Sadhu begged God to save him and walked out softly. He succeeded. The beast had not moved. But once outside he was filled with remorse. He was a child of God. He should not have walked out. The tiger should have yielded to him. So he prayed for this, re-entered the cave, and this time the tiger walked out leaving Sadhu alone.

But the marvel is that we have power over not only evil forces, but also over good angels. Jacob fought with a good angel and prevailed (Gen. 32:24, Hos. 12:4). Our heavenly Bridegroom Himself says to the faithful soul, "Turn away thine eyes from me, for they have overcome me" (Song of Solomon 6:5). The faithful soul is of such irresistible beauty in God's sight that He is conquered the moment He hears our voice. Jesus promises, "Ye shall ask what ye will, and it shall be done unto you" (John 15:7), which means that we will have the victory in every conversation with God.

I believe in God. I have this power. I am *something*. And here in my prison cell, which might as well be a psychiatric ward since to a certain extent I have long since gone mad, knowing what the grace of Christ has made of me, I will dare to sing the song that expresses what every Christian thinks in the depths of his heart but does not dare to say in so many words: "Then sings my soul, my Saviour God to Thee, 'How great I am, how great I am.'"

That I feel unworthy and weak does not count. When Zacharias, the father of St. John the Baptist, hesitated to believe the promise of God saying, "I am an old man" (Luke 1:18), he received this reply from the divine messenger: "I am Gabriel." In Hebrew the word "I" has two forms, *Ani* and the amplified *Anohi*. Somewhere there might be a little "I" named "Richard." But it has been amplified by angels and by Christ Himself, and now it is great.

Mock me as much as you like, torturers. Your abuses have had just the opposite effect from what you expected. You have not humiliated me. You have shown me my greatness.

"I will praise thee; for I am fearfully and wonderfully made" (Psalms 139:14), says David, uniting words of self-admiration with words of gratitude towards the One to whom we owe our greatness.

I thank you, God, that I am great. Amen.

# BEWARE OF NARCISSISM

DEAR BRETHREN AND SISTERS

My blurred reason swings like a pendulum from one extreme to the other. I know that my sermons are not well balanced. Yesterday I was full of admiration for my great "I". Such a sermon I would never have delivered from a pulpit. If it reaches you from my prison cell, take it with reservations. Not all sermons are the expression of objective truth. Sometimes they just reflect a transitory mood of the preacher. Just as a song is not a succession of single notes or chords but is heard in between, unwritten, so God's revelation is not in any one sermon, but runs as a theme between sermons.

Now I feel just the opposite of the way I felt yesterday. How could I admire myself?

If there were a human being with the right to self-admiration it was the Virgin Mary. She was of a purity which all the lilies on earth and all the stars in the sky could envy. She was filled with passionate love for God. I do not know any human being who might have been as God-like as Mary.

She had the dual honour of being a princess and a virgin, not only in body but also in spirit. She was a great poet. Her song is outstanding. Referring to her words, "Henceforth all generations shall call me blessed" (Luke 1:48), Spurgeon said, "I suppose Protestant generations are among the 'all' who ought to call her

101

blessed" (Charles Spurgeon, *Christ's Names and Titles*).

Legend says that it was St. Luke's hobby to paint pictures of Mary. One is supposedly in Italy. This legend might not be true. But it is certain that Luke painted a beautiful picture of her in his Gospel. To contemplate this picture is ennobling.

An angel spoke directly to her, but she never said the foolish words which I said yesterday, "How great I am!" While Gabriel showed her his respect, she called herself a "handmaid of the Lord" and was humble in her dealing with the divine messenger. She responded, "Be it unto me according to thy word" (Luke 1:38). Luther writes "Mary, after the annunciation, does not boast, does not shout, 'I have become the mother of God,' she asks for no honour, but works in the house like before, milks the cows, cooks, washes dishes, sweeps and is busy with little, despised things, as a maid or housewife should do and as if she would disdain the great gifts and graces. Women and neighbours don't consider her as something higher than before. Neither did she ask for it but she remained a poor woman among the little people."

She had understood the full depth of his words, "The power of the Highest shall overshadow thee" (Luke 1:35). When God intervenes in the life of a man, he begins to love the shadow. The bride in Song of Solomon (2:3) says about her beloved, "I sat down under his shadow with great delight."

"In the shadow of his hand has he hid me," says Isaiah (49:2).

Self-admiration is false. How the wardens and officers take pride in their uniforms. They are as sure that they prepare the future happiness of mankind as their enemies are sure that the Communists are devils. Every nation, religion, party and caste sees only ideal qualities in itself and chops off the heads of others in order to appear taller.

How horribly wrong were my feelings yesterday. I was enamoured of myself. It was only after I delivered the sermon that I remembered Romans 15:3, "Christ pleased not himself." He would not allow a young man to call Him "good". Neither did He have a bias for the religion of His childhood. He called the temple a den of thieves. I do not think He is much in love with what is commonly called the Christian Church either, although it bears His name. He sees His picture painted on walls and stained glass windows. Inside, a priest or pastor fulfils the role of a businessman, and even this he does not do well. Proof of it is the fact that the "grocers" who attempt to sell spiritual commodities increasingly lose customers.

Jesus did not please Himself. The virgin Mary did not. Should I congratulate myself because I did the Lord the kindness of repenting of my sins and receiving His forgiveness?

Did I even really repent? The Bible speaks of sackcloth and ashes as the outward evidence of true repentance. I try in vain to remember even one acquaintance who ever repented like this. What man is there who, in order to think uprightly, to believe only what is based on fact, to have faith and not credulity, to avoid any uncontrolled thoughts, to judge dispassionately, in a disinterested manner, resisting any pressure, hatred, preference, fear or illusion, even if this meant being stripped of everything – what man chooses to be clothed in nondescript rags and to have, instead of a warm fireside, only the ashes of a fire quenched long before?

Where is the man who has repented so deeply that he is willing to renounce even eternity if he thought it a hindrance to the fulfilment of the Kingdom? Who has repented so whole-heartedly that Jesus and only Jesus counts?

We repent of our sins and then commit the sin of admiring our repentance, instead of repenting of it as of a trespass because it is superficial.

Yesterday my torturers secured my legs with a rope. Then they wedged a stick between the bonds. The stick was turned until the rope, tightened to the breaking point, bit deeply into the flesh. Their torture prejudices us against them so that we cannot concede that they are right in their thinking. Holiness is the same thing as ideal Communism. Holiness means to have nothing of your own, no material goods, no sin, no righteousness of your own, not even repentance of your own. Holiness is perfect communion or sharing with Jesus and the saints. Our lives should have been Jesus and only Jesus. Then the Communists would have become Christians.

An artist sang *Rigoletto* badly. People booed her. Indignant, she said to her colleagues, "What an uneducated audience! They dare to jeer Verdi!" They did not jeer the composer but the performer. I believe that those who beat us opposed not Christ but us Christians who admired ourselves without reason.

Every man's energy budget is fixed. The more he spends on one activity the less remains for something else. It is vain to spend energy on self and self-admiration when we need all our energy for things of eternal value.

I know that today's sermon is just the opposite of yesterday's. A pastor would never dare contradict himself so obviously in the pulpit. He is under compulsion to be consistent in order to be respected. But I am free simply because I am in a solitary cell. Contradictory thoughts and sentiments pass through my mind just as they do through yours. I give you all of me.

The whole philosophy of the Christian mystics is contained in the following parable. Once there were three beautiful birds in the same tree. The one in the topmost branches was serene, enthroned in majesty, immersed in its own glory. In the lower branches, the second was agitated because the fruit it tasted was bitter, while the third found the fruit tasty, but the sweetness lasted only as long as the food was on its little tongue. In their common disappointment, the two latter birds hopped higher and higher on the branches until they approached the serene bird. Losing themselves in its glory, they discovered that there had never been three birds but only one – the majestic one.

I told you in one sermon my feeling of being exalted, in another my humiliation. While composing the first I felt well, but alas, for such a short moment. Humiliation on the other hand is bitter. With my false glory and worthless humility I came to the divine bird that wishes to gather her little ones under her wings. Here both states of heart disappeared. There is none other than the one Jesus. All the rest is illusion, not worth mentioning. Amen.

# THE SHADOW HAS BEEN BROUGHT BACKWARD

DEAR BRETHREN AND SISTERS

King Hezekiah of the Jews was sick. The prophet Isaiah had promised him that he would recover and, yielding to his request, promised him a sign that this would happen. Now, Hezekiah had a sundial. Isaiah prayed, and the Lord "brought the shadow ten degrees backward" (II Kings 20:11).

Many find it difficult to believe that the shadow went backward ten hours, but the Bible does not claim this. It is written "ten degrees", not "ten hours". The degrees could have been minutes, or even less.

Neither must we suppose that, for the performance of this miracle, the earth would have had to turn backward on its axis, contrary to its natural course. The phenomenon could have occurred by means of refraction. A ray of light is refracted from a straight line by passing through a medium of another density. Because of the refracting power of the atmosphere, the sun, when rising or setting, seems to be higher above the horizon than it really is. The miracle could have been performed by means of refraction.

The Jewish sundial had a unique form. In II Kings 9:13 it is written that the friends of Jehu, when he was proclaimed king, "took every man his garment, and put it under him on the top of the stairs." The Targum of Rabbi Joseph (a Targum is an Aramaic translation of a book) here used the words *lidrag sheaiya*, meaning the hour-steps. The division of time was shown by a shadow projected on stone steps, gradually ascending to a certain height.

This also gives meaning to the title of Psalms 120 through 134, "Songs of Degrees". They are Psalms through whose meditation you can advance in time, but also return to former times on certain occasions.

Try to understand what a gift Hezekiah received. Not only did the shadow on the sundial return but also the time indicated by the shadow. He was younger. A few minutes or hours were as if they had not passed yet. All hours and days belong to God, and He can let you relive today an hour from thirty years ago.

At Cana, Jesus changed the water into "good wine" (John 2:10). Good wine is old wine. So Jesus changed water not into a liquid which immediately became wine, but a liquid which had become wine long before. When a man is converted, not only are his present and future transformed, but also his past. He is changed into a man who has always been elect and righteous in God's eyes.

The shadow has gone backward on my sundial, too. I am a child again. Life is before me as if I had not lived it yet, and now I am free to change decisions that I think were wrong. Hindsight is always better than foresight. At my present age I know better what I should have done in childhood and in youth. Now I can go back and do it. Time is reversible for the faithful. We sing the songs of degrees and ascend and descend freely on the steps of time.

I am eight years old again. Until then I had never heard about Christ. On this particular occasion I came from school with another child. He stopped before a Catholic church and asked me to wait while he delivered a message to the priest. I preferred to enter with him and so found myself in a Christian church for the first time.

I understood absolutely nothing of what I observed. I saw someone hanging on a cross and wondered what horrible deeds He must have committed to be punished like that. I saw a beautiful lady with a child in her arms. You will say that I saw only the statues. It might be. I remember seeing the Crucified and a Lady. Now that the shadow has gone back on the sundial, I see that my memory is correct. Only blind men see crosses and statues in churches. There was the lady and a multitude of other beings looking benign, calm, loving (as people never look ordinarily). I wondered who these were and why they stood in this half-dark house in complete silence.

The boy spoke with the priest. I had not the slightest idea what a priest was. But this then came to me and caressed me on my head. Why don't priests do this more often? We bring our children to pastors that they might *teach* them. Children were brought to Jesus that He might *touch* them. The right touch of a man who knows how to bless is worth a thousand teachings.

He asked me, "What can I do for you, little fellow?" I answered, "Nothing. I just entered with my comrade." Then this priest (I found out after almost fifty years that his name was Giuseppe Cavane) told me, "I am the disciple of One who has taught me never to allow anybody to pass near me without doing him at least a little bit of good. It is hot outside. Would you allow me to bring you a cup of cold water?" I have drunk many beverages since then, but none tasted like this water.

I was stupid then. I left the priest without questioning

him further. But now I am again a boy of eight. And I sit down near the priest and ask him more and more about this mysterious One who does good to everybody and teaches people to do the same. I would have heard that He is the One crucified for His goodness, that the beautiful lady was His mother, and that the beings with wings are his angelic host. Today I can become a disciple of Jesus from the age of eight.

I don't think that I would have listened to the priest very long. He probably would not have spoken much. It is so wrong to interrupt the silence of churches even with sermons and splendid music. Often nothing more is needed than just looking to Jesus. If he had explained to me that it was for my sins He suffered, it would have been enough.

And now I stand near the sad mother at the foot of the cross.

When I first saw her standing there, a scene flashed through my mind. I had been sick with typhus at a very early age. The doctor, who could not possibly imagine that I knew French, said to my mother in this language, "There is no hope. The child will die." I asked my mother, "What is death?" and she began to weep. She did not tell me. She did not know herself that it means a return to God. But Mary knows. She is sad, but confident. She looks much younger than He.

A sword pierces her heart. I will take it out of her heart. But how? I am so small and weak. Oh, if the shadow could advance faster on the sundial. I wish to grow, just enough to be able to do what I wish. Then I would ask her how we could help Jesus not to hang on the cross.

Mary, speak now and tell me that the whole dreadful scene has passed, that He is resurrected. How strange hat I should have grown up as a Jew among Christian children and yet no one ever told me this until now. But He did suffer, and she, too.

I can make decisions anew. I will never again leave this building. How wrong it was to start Christian activities, to become a missionary, to accomplish rituals. One thing is needed: to sit quietly in this hushed place and to live the oneness.

A Russian soldier told us about an atheist lecturer who had come to an underground meeting. The Christian preacher asked him at the exit, "How many do you think were here?" He answered, "A hundred." The preacher replied, "This is what you saw. Actually, we were one, one soul and one heart. We are one person who bears the name 'hundred'. We are one who soars towards heaven, and heaven inclines towards us with all its beauties. If you could feel for one moment the rapture of this oneness, not only with our fellowmen but with the whole creation and with God, you would leave everything in the world for it."

No more is needed than to be just one. I can start life again. It will no longer lead an active but a contemplative life: the quiet enjoyment of oneness.

But no, it seems I am not made for this.

The priest in the church teaches me the who and the what of life. I grow up in the Church. The shadow on the sundial advances again, but slowly. I have time. The Church, a loving mother and teacher, also shows me how to lead the Christian fight. In my other life I had to guess at it and made many mistakes.

We know from the episodes of Gethsemane that the disciples of Jesus were armed. It is natural to have defensive weapons when you are threatened. Peter carried a sword but had no idea how to handle it. He cut off the right ear of the high priest's servant. What was the good of that? A policeman with a cut ear can still arrest your beloved. Don't fight – but if you have decided to fight, hit your adversary right on the head. Jesus then points out that the sword is not a toy, that you can perish from it. Whoever has inhibitions about the enemies of the Church and cuts off only ears had better keep his sword in its sheath.

God said, "The seed of the woman shall bruise thy (the serpent's) head." Instead of this, we sometimes tickle the serpent on the belly and make him laugh. It is all because we have not learned the "how". But I am young again and learn to handle the sword of the Spirit.

I have terrible pain. I seem to bear an aching skull, not a head. But this is from my other life. Now the sundial has gone back. It has reversed itself only for me. A whole generation of Christian fighters can arise. Those who have neglected their duty or have fulfilled it wrongly can make things right as of forty, fifty, or sixty years ago.

David was a man in whom God was pleased. But listen to his last words before he died. They were about Shimei, a man who had cursed God's anointed. David said to Solomon, "His hoar head bring thou down to the grave with blood. So David slept with his fathers" (1 Kings 2:9, 10). From the beginning of the Christian life to its last breath, the enemies of God have to be destroyed. Every man meeting you is given the dramatic alternative: either he will be saved or he will perish – if not by your hand, then through the faithful word which you told him and which he did not receive.

I had so many quarrels in my other life, even with brethren. I pace thorugh my cell humming in Hebrew from memory the Psalms of Degrees. Now "I am for peace" (Psalm 120:7), "My soul is even as a weaned child" (Psalm 131:2).

In a democracy you must win the majority of people

or of a congregation to see your will fulfilled. Not so with God. It is enough that two should agree on earth as touching anything, and it shall be done for them by the Heavenly Father (Matt. 18:19).

But if couples disagree about contrary matters, don't they have to argue with each other? Now, by hindsight I can see that it is not necessary. The Father has unlimited time. He can move the shadow on the sundial forward and backward as many times as He likes. He also has a multitude of worlds. All couples will see their will fulfilled even if they differ.

Last night I dreamt that a monk complained to me that his superior was wicked, a kind of Torquemada. He told me this with joy, explaining that his superior, through making him suffer innocently, had accomplished something similar to opening a large bank account for him. All the cheques he draws are covered because God looks on the credit side. He has suffered.

In my former life I had shunned many sufferings. I had preferred to prevaricate rather than endure pain. A new opportunity has been given to me. Here you have my body and soul, all those who wish to hurt me. Do me a favour. I have a new life before me. It will be one of suffering, of renunciation.

I am free here of the necessity of being consistent in my preaching. This need causes preachers to leave great potentialities unused. No one is all of a piece. The part that you repress is also valuable and could also praise God.

In his autobiography, Charles Darwin notes that, as his interests became increasingly absorbed in science, he lost the pleasure in poetry and the plays of Shakespeare which had formerly been a prominent feature of his life. He might have done better in these than in biology. In freedom I, too, had given up parts of my interests in life.

Here everything is aflame.

How should I continue this sermon and how should I end it coming back to its main subject, the sundial? But why must the end of a sermon correspond to its beginning? Why must it have a logical conclusion?

I am tired now of preaching. Life will go on even without a continuation of my sermon. Good night, dear brethren. Amen.

# A RELIGION WITHOUT GOD

DEAR BRETHREN AND SISTERS

There are many things we know that we don't *know* we know. The Lord said to His disciples, "Whither I go ye know, and the way ye know," to which Thomas replied, "Lord, we know not whither thou goest; and how can we know the way?" (John 14:4, 5). Thomas knew but did not know that he knew. Jesus said of John the Baptist that he was Elias, the prophet of old, who was to come. John, when asked, said that he was not Elias. This man did not know the essence of his own being. How could he have known what his being knew?

It is only in the narrow limits of the circumstances in which I now find myself – alone for years in a solitary cell without any book or any impression from the outside, dependent upon my own inner resources to occupy myself – that I find a large unexplored field existing in my mind to which I have access.

Without any material to read, without anything happening to stimulate my mind, I think new and strange thoughts. I am conscious of knowing more than I knew before. From whence did I acquire this new knowledge? It is not through drawing further conclusions from what I knew before, through a process of reasoning. Who can reason when hungry and beaten? No, I had known these things for a long time. But one thing was missing: I had not *known* that I knew them.

114

Plato was right: "To know is to recognise."

Being alone is the prerequisite for plumbing your own depths. I would be much alone, aloof from you, the most dearly beloved, even if I were not in prison. Jesus said, "That the world may know that I love the Father," I leave the world and go to the Father (John 14:28, 31). How would the villagers know that the bridegroom loved the bride if he amused himself with his friends while she was kept waiting for him? Jesus has to leave all his friends so that they may know He loves the Father. Loving Him, He reveals to you His mysteries.

Do not believe the pastors who are constantly busy around you. Believe those who declare, "Hereafter I will not talk much with you" (John 14:30), as they contemplate their own depths. They might very well discover ultimate truths. You may not be aware of the fact. Their faces will not shine, because they will veil them as did Moses. They do not speak of these hidden experiences.

I am on my way to this contemplative state.

Last night I dreamt that an Orthodox Jew with a beard and curls asked me, "What is the other world?"

I answered, "It is where one has the answer. This world is the world of asking questions."

But I am already at the border of the other world. I begin to have the replies.

We have our first reply in the Bible. But scholars know that the Bible is like reality as defined by Planck and Heisenberg in modern physics, a wave of probabilities. You can never say what and where an elementary particle is and what it will do. You handle it by working on probabilities.

As for the Bible, we do not have such a book. There are countless manuscripts with many variations among them. The Hebrew language itself is very imprecise. It has no tenses. The same form of the verb can be used as a curse or only as a declaration that something bad may happen.

For example, in Psalm 83:15 one and the same word can be translated as an imprecatory prayer, "Persecute them with thy tempest," or as a prediction, "Thou wilt persecute them with thy tempest."

A single Hebrew word sometimes has contrary meanings. *Baruh* means "blessed" and "cursed". *Kedoshim* means "saints" and "Sodomites". Much is left to the arbitrary decision of the translator.

There are parallel texts in many parts of the Hebrew: the *Ketub*, the writing, and the *Keri*, the rule of reading, which might differ greatly from the former. In II Kings 20:4, for example, is the *hatser*, which means "yard". But the masoretic rule is to read *hair*, which means "the town". The difference is great. In the first case, the prophet Isaiah is very near King Hezekiah, in the latter he is far away. The *Ketub* plus the *Keri* form the Hebrew Bible.

The situation is similar in the Greek. We can translate the word *afes* so that the Biblical text reads, "Forgive us our trespasses," or "Leave us our trespasses," in which case we would have a prayer to continue in our favourite sin.

Most of us read the Bible in translation. Every translation is a treason, even the translation of sentiments into words, but especially the translation of Hebrew or Greek words into another language or another mentality.

For the Nunggubaya in Australia the expression "Holy Spirit" could not be translated. They have nothing similar. So the translators have used instead "the pretty witch doctor in the sky". Consequently, in their Bible they read that when Jesus was baptised, a pretty witch doctor descended upon Him from the sky, and that those who believe and are baptised will have this pretty witch doctor on their side, which seems very curious to us.

But even the English is faulty. The words "Holy Spirit" are as curious and as inadequate as the words "pretty witch doctor," because "holy" comes from a word meaning "whole" and "spirit" comes from the Latin *spirare* meaning "to breathe"; therefore, "Holy Spirit" means to breathe deeply involving the whole lung.

In Mark 16:16, Jesus said, "He that believeth and is baptised shall be saved." For the Nunggubaya the expression "saved" was translated *aniladi-in*, which means in their language "to receive a hard job." So whosoever believes will receive a hard job. The missionaries wondered why they preached and preached about being saved and had no converts!

Even in the original, the answers of the Bible are like the answers of science: every answer raises new problems.

But I am bound to this world only by a thin umbilical cord. My thoughts belong to the world of answers. I have always had them in me. I had not known that I had known them.

There exists a world in which man has no God, because the separation has ceased. The Godhead exists. It created man. And man had a God. But when man returns to his Source there is union. In this context, you see that the holiest book in the Bible is Esther, in which the word "God" never occurs. For the obvious, no words or names are needed. Here you understand the Lord's prayer, "Hallowed be thy name." The original Greek is *"Aghiatheto to onoma su,"* which, literally translated, means, "May thy name be taken away from the earth," so that instead of many names we would have the unnamed reality. (In Greek "*a*" = "un," "*ghea*" = "earth").

The Bible mentions a multitude of holy books inspired to proclaim the name of God. They have been lost. We no longer have them. They disappeared to indicate that there is a higher reality than a mere book: the ultimate reality about which it can only babble.

In Esther the word "God" is never mentioned. Not even in Esther 4:3, in which we read that there was fasting, weeping, wailing, but no prayer to God. His help was taken for granted. Not many words are needed in intercourse between the "me" and "me". Jesus promises conquerors that they will sit with Him on His throne, just as He has conquered and now sits on His Father's throne. What God does a being have who sits on the throne of God from which worlds are created and ruled?

God's name is blasphemed because of our sins. His reality is beyond attack. In Him everyone lives and moves. There is no one to attack Him. The Communists rebel against His name, against what they fancy Him to be, against the manner in which we have represented Him. But there exists no real rebellion against Him. The Communists are not worse than Satan. Yet Satan himself could not touch Job without asking humble permission from God.

There also exists this sphere of the one reality, without an "I" and a "He". The book of Esther is its best expression.

I know only that this last reality is terribly, unbearably harsh. I know it, therefore I cannot live with it.

I prefer the first day of faith, when I knew that God is the "God of pardons" (Neh. 9:17, in the original). But how can one receive forgiveness when he lives on the knowledge of unity with Godhead?

Having a God, you can reduce your obligations. The law of Moses prescribed that every Jew should give half a shekel to the temple annually. We read in the book of Nehemiah that the Jews were allowed to give only a third, contrary to the law. They had become poor after long years of slavery in Babylon. The laws of God are not implacable. The laws of reality, on the contrary, know no bargaining. When you fall from a height, you smash your head and that is that. When the clock runs out, you die.

So I prefer to turn off the knowledge of what I know and say like Luther, "I will have nothing to do with an absolute God. I will not try to study Him as God. I know tht I cannot look at the sun. I must have a tinted glass to look through. I must have the person of the God-man to take away the blinding glory of the invisible God, invisible because too bright for my eyes to gaze upon. I must have God in Christ. I will not try to study anything else."

But perhaps we are unjust towards the book of Esther. Is the notion of God really absent from it? It is written in the Talmud, "In every place where you find the imprint of men's feet, there am I." Mordecai and his cousin Esther have left deep imprints in history. God *is* in the book. Amen.

# SHOULD I PRAY TO BE FREED?

MY GOD

I know how to say "Our Father" but do not know what to add. Should I ask you for freedom? If so, why?

Once a businessman from Boston told Mark Twain, "I have attained much in life, but one great desire has remained unfulfilled, that is, to make a pilgrimage to the Holy Land."

"What will you do there?" asked Twain.

"I would like to ascend Mount Sinai and there read the Ten Commandments in Hebrew as they were given by God."

Mark Twain replied, "That's too complicated. Would it not be much more comfortable to remain in Boston and fulfil the Ten Commandments?"

It is not necessary to go to holy places in order to be pleasing to Thee. But neither is it necessary to be at liberty. Which commandment could I keep better in freedom than in a prison cell? Why should I move around? The lily stays in the same place and exhales its perfume.

What does it count that I am alone? I had this problem when I was pastor of the church. I had inherited from my predecessor a church with a small attendance. In the beginning I was sad about it. But then I quieted my heart and told the brethren, "Instead of worrying about those who are absent, let each of us multiply his zeal and fervour and love. It is for these that God looks out. If He finds one man with as much love as only a hundred men would normally have, He is satisfied."

In my solitary cell I am undisturbed. I can work on my character to develop the virtues of thousands.

I will not pray to be freed.

The apostles were afraid during a storm and wanted to be rescued. Jesus fulfilled their pleasure, and so they escaped drowning. In exchange they were later martyred. In this world rescue from temporary troubles cannot have any other result.

I will not pray for peace of heart. I have some kind of peace.

Conscience is like a triangle of metal in my heart. If I am good, it stands still and does not bother me. If I am bad it begins to circle and the angles hurt. If I am very bad, the angles lose their sharpness through much circling, and again I am not bothered. At this moment I am not troubled. What peace I have I cannot judge for myself. Neither do I have anyone with whom I can consult.

But either way I know that I am loved, because I suffer, and it is written, "He that has suffered in the flesh has ceased from sin" (1 Peter 4:1).

In his book about the Virgin Mary's song, Luther tells of a vision. Three virgins knelt before an altar. During the service a beautiful young man appeared and hugged the first girl and kissed her. He did not kiss the second, but smiled at her with great friendliness. As for the third, he hit her and pulled her hair. With this the young man disappeared.

Later the vision was explained. The first virgin symbolises the selfish, unregenerate souls. God must do much good to them. He must fulfil their will towards them, not His own. They cannot live without receiving many blessings from God.

The second virgin represents those who have started to serve God but still need, at least from time to time, a friendly gesture from Him. They cannot simply love Him without expecting anything in return. They cannot simply love Him, whatever He does and however He behaves.

The third virgin, the Cinderella, represents the saintly soul who loves God without any ulterior motive. She simply *loves*. She is happy if He does good to others. Mary would have sung the same beautiful Magnificat if she had been told that another girl, yes, one who despised her, had been chosen by God to be the mother of the Lord. Such do not need the caresses of the Lord. They are happy to bear their cross for Him and pass through a dark night of the soul. If He wishes to abandon them while they undergo suffering, they do not complain. Everything is right only if it is His good pleasure. For these souls God multiplies the chastisings. "Whom the Lord loves he chastises, and scourges every son whom he receives" (Heb. 12:6).

A great Master like You would not scourge someone personally. Therefore, the Communists might be Your tools for this purpose. If one were to judge by the number of beatings I have received, I must be very much beloved.

That would be good, but if I knew it and took undue satisfaction in it, I would not be like the third virgin. In the end, atheists also pass through suffering. The whole matter is too complicated for my poor reason.

The simplest thing is just to leave it and remain in peace, not trying to distinguish with my blurred mind if it is the right kind of peace or not.

I will sit still in this my hidden cell and look to You, the hidden God, without bothering You with any request.

I have given up the popularisation of religion as contained in the creed, which speaks about God only as a creator. You are also the preserver and the destroyer. If it is not You who destroys, who does? You are not simply the Creator who left creation to develop as it would; You are the Creator of all things, including the angel called the Destroyer (Ex. 12:23). You also created the microbes that kill. You are described as destroyer in Lamentations 2. You continually destroy lives that You have created. "The Lord kills and makes alive. He brings down to the grave, and brings up" (1 Sam. 2:6). Both these activities bring You honour. I love You whatever You choose to do.

In Maramuresh there is a place called "the humorous cemetery", which expresses even today what the Dacians of history (the ancestors of Romanians) believed about death. They dressed in white and rejoiced when someone died. On every cross in this cemetery is carved some joyful scene from the life of the buried man. They knew that You destroyed this life in order to create another one.

I owe you the happiness which I had in my family and church. From Your hand I also receive the destruction of this happiness, which was necessary in order to replace it with the happiness of sitting in a subterranean cell, completely free of everything that disturbs, and of looking to the hidden God; the happiness of having passed from the holy place of the temple to the most holy place.

When Gehazi asked the Shunammite woman after her son had died, "Is it well with the child?" she answered, "It is well" (II Kings 4:26). She would have said the same words on the day of the child's birth.

If I get tired looking at You and my mind is distraught, it does not matter. You never slumber nor sleep. You look at me.

When my son was small he asked me, "Father, what should I do? I am bored."

I told him, "Think about God."

His reply was, "Why should I think about Him with this little head of mine? Let Him think about me with His big head."

The apparatus at the great observatory of Mount Palomar is so sensitive that the heartbeat of the astronomer disturbs it. The simplest thing is to efface oneself completely, not to be bothered about what happens. I think it is never reality which bothers us; we are bothering reality. I will stop doing so. I have You as Father in Heaven. I lovingly called You "Father". This is all. No other prayer is needed, and no request.

I will not ask to be freed. Amen.

# MANKIND IS INNOCENT

GOD

Mankind is innocent, if looked upon from a certain perspective. An X-ray of a pretty girl's cranium doesn't look any better than that of a gorilla.

The Bible is full of good news, including Paul's declaration, "All have sinned and come short of the glory of God" (Rom. 3:23).

If this is true, then before I ever sinned I was a man much sinned against. "There is none righteous, no, not one" (v. 10). Thousands of ancestors have transmitted their heredity to me through the genes, programming almost all of my future characteristics. And not one of these ancestors was righteous. Then all my heredity must be terribly bad. I have been educated by grandparents, parents, teachers. Of what quality were they? The same apostle says, "There is none that does good, no, not one" (v. 12). I did not have one to give me the right instruction.

"Behold, I was shapen in iniquity," says the Psalmist (51:5). Since when does any reasonable person hold it against a statue for being ugly? Only the sculptor is responsible. "All have sinned." Absolutely every man with whom I have come in contact since early childhood has sinned against me. I was buffeted to and fro long before I said or did the first wrong thing. So, God, looks upon me not so much as a sinner but as a man sinned

against, who, under continual provocation and surrounded only by bad examples, commits some iniquitous
deed. Even a human court acquits in such a case.

I used to ask people who confessed some sin, "Tell me
something about your parents and grandparents."
Often enough it was to give them some relief. One had
quarrelled. His parents had been choleric, quarrelsome.
A preacher had fallen repeatedly into adultery and
justified it on the basis that Abraham, too, had been a
polygamist. He had not realised the connection between
this and the fact that his father had been jailed for a
sexual crime. It helped one who fought against the
impulse of gambling to know that his father had been a
compulsive gambler.

It is worthwhile trying to learn the beginnings of a
man's sin. There is always some seducer, some bad book,
some tendentious movie. A mountain of sin has fallen
upon us and crushed us morally before we ever sin.

"All have sinned" – this is the comforting news that
You give us. It is not that I alone happen to be a wicked
evil-doer or that I alone, though living in a pure
paradise and surrounded only by angels and saints, have
started to sin out of pleasure or perversity.

Nor is it only the influence of other men that has made
me sin. I belong to nature, a nature that is not morally
neutral. "The creature was made subject to vanity"
(Rom. 8:20). It is in the "bondage of corruption" (v. 21).
There is something in my body, in my very nerves, that
compels me to sin.

I will remind You of an extreme case.

Robert Ledrue, who had been in his youth one of the
foremost detectives of France, was given the assignment
to investigate a murder that occurred in Le Havre. A
man who bathed in the sea at night was shot when he
came out of the water. Nobody knew the motive for the

murder. But the murderer had left prints in the sand and a bullet in the victim.

Ledrue investigated, went to the head of the police, and asked to be arrested. He had found out that he himself had been the murderer. It was a unique case. The bullet had been shot from a special kind of revolver possessed by only four men. He was one of them. The imprints in the sand showed that the murderer lacked the big toe on the right foot. Ledrue's had been amputated. The detective was sure that he was the murderer but did not remember having killed anyone and knew no motive for doing so.

He asked to be kept permanently under surveillance by police. They discovered that he was a somnambulist. Later he shot at another person while wandering around at night, completely unconscious of what he was doing. Fortunately, the police had filled his revolver with harmless bullets. After shooting, he returned quietly to his home and went to bed, with no idea of what he had done.

For murder while in a state of somnambulism, Ledrue was sentenced to lifelong isolation on a solitary farm under police surveillance.

What is our state when we commit crimes? Jesus said of His executioners, "They know not what they do." St. Peter said, "Ye killed the Prince of life . . . I know that through ignorance ye did it, as did also your rulers" (Acts 3:15, 17).

How much is a man responsible for what he does? St. Paul wrote, "The evil which I would not, that I do. Now if I do that I would not, it is no more I that do it, but sin that dwells in me" (Rom. 7:19, 20). In this passage sin appears as a foreign intruder against whom I am helpless, just as I am helpless against a massive attack of tuberculosis microbes. It is not something I have courted deliberately with my reason and will.

Benjamin was found with a stolen cup in his sack, put there not by himself but by Joseph's servants (Gen. 44:2). So what appears as my sin, the stolen cup in my character, is the result of innumerable actions of men, all sinners, who shaped my life, all abetted by what has become disorderly in nature. The apostle continues: "I find then a law [who has established it?], that, when I would do good, evil is present with me . . . I see another law in my members, warring against the law of my mind" (Rom. 7: 21, 23).

Sin and guilt are not the same things. I can commit a sin without being guilty of it, as for example under extreme coercion, inner irresistible impulse, complete ignorance, etc. You have told us, "There is nothing covered that shall not be revealed" (Luke 12:2). This is a fact of everyday experience. In our dreams when rightly analysed, in daydreams, in slips of the tongue and under hypnosis, hidden things become manifest. They will also become manifest in the other world. All the ugly deeds will be known there. But we don't have to be afraid. There they will be known by beings who are no longer as we are now. Everybody will be full of understanding, insight, compassion, and power to repair wrongs. Sometimes a child weeps over a catastrophe that has happened to him. Father observes. However, to him it is not a catastrophe, and so he makes the broken toy work again.

Jesus referred to sinners as sick men who need a physician instead of a judge. He heals sin with a medicine, His own blood shed for us.

I was in the same cell with a man sentenced to death for numerous sadistic murders. He confessed to me and answered my questions. His father had been an alcoholic. The only remembrance he had of him was that he came home drunk, beat him and his mother, stole all the money that his mother had earned by sewing, and left home to drink again. When the child was hungry, his mother would beat him for crying.

At the age of fourteen, attracted by the uniform and by songs that seemed to make sense, he joined a Fascist anti-Semitic organisation. For this, the royal government put him in prison. Since there were no separate juvenile facilities, he mingled with all sorts of criminals, who thenceforth were his educators. Though the royal regime was later overturned, the Communists never forgave anyone. And so for the crime of being a Fascist at the age of fourteen, he was imprisoned again and beaten. Then he was offered the chance of being freed if he would torture other prisoners to death. He accepted the offer. It was his only chance for survival. After he had served as henchman for a long time, the same Communist masters sentenced him to death.

If you were to ask me today, "What is the sum of your experience with mankind?" my immediate reply would be, "Father, they are not guilty; they don't know what they do." I would include my torturers in this appreciation. We are meant to be the defenders of men, not their accusers. We even have to defend desperate cases. To accuse is the devil's business.

Every fibre of my heart believes in strict determinism. Omar Khayyam wrote:

> 'Tis all a chequer board of nights and days
> Where destiny with men for pieces plays,
> Hither and thither moves and mates and slays,
> And one by one back in the closet lays.

Luther once said that whoever erased the words "free will" from the human dictionary would render the

# THE ENCOUNTER WITH LUCIFER

DEAR BRETHREN AND SISTERS

To know God is not enough. We must know the enemy, too.

Even Jesus did not avoid a face-to-face discussion with the devil. If we don't bring to the bar of reason the temptations of Satan, they will enter the depths of the subconscious, where the great decisions are made, and ravage the soul.

I would not recommend this to everyone, but I have studied the tenets of the Satanist sects. One must have special grace to tackle this subject and not be overcome. Satan's words seemed good and were convincing to Eve, though she lived in God's paradise. How much more do they lure us, her fallen progeny. Our sinful nature responds all too readily to the great claims of Satan and his followers. They can be studied only with a constant struggle to resist their baleful influence on one's character.

I remember the chill that went down my spine when I read the secret formula disclosed only to initiates during the introduction to the third degree: "Let my will happen in all things." The formula was not new to me. It tapped into the huge drive for self-assertion which we all have in us. It is just the contrary of the teaching of our Lord: "Whosoever will come after me, let him deny himself" (Mark 8:34).

Human nature says "no" to this command of Jesus. But if the grace of God comes and you are inclined to fulfil it, be aware that Satan can disguise himself and make of conversion to Christ an initiation into the Satanic rite. If you were to express in clear words what happens in such a case, it would be as follows: "I must be a man with a very strong 'I' to be able to decide even the rejection of the 'I', the only great treasure I possess. So let *my* will happen in religion, too. My will is to deny myself."

Afterwards you can go to great lengths of self-denial. You can go even as far as giving away all your possessions and being burned at the stake for your ideals. It is the "I" that will have chosen poverty or martyrdom. Without knowing it, you will have been faithful to the formula of initiation: "Let my will happen in all things – even in matters regarding my relationship with Christ."

"Deny yourself" is one of the many laws of Scripture. They have not been given to be fulfilled. As a man born in sin, you cannot fulfil them. You can only take cognisance of them, seeing in them, as in a mirror, how far away you are from what is beautiful and right. You then acknowledge your sinfulness, at which point Christ can work in you. *He* changes you from glory to glory. But every human work you engage in by yourself, even a very holy one, is extremely dangerous.

Every day I have to decide whether to yield to torture or not, whether to deny Christ or not. It might be not a consecrated attitude but a devilish one to say, "Let my will be done, and my will is that I should be a hero of the faith."

The Lord wants some to be such heroes but he also allowed Peter to pass through moments of cowardice and then return with repentance, thus giving an example throughout the centuries to Christians who might fall in times of persecution that they can rise again.

I decide nothing about what I will do tomorrow at the interrogation.

A rabbi once stood at the window of his study and called to the first Jew who went by. He asked him, "Suppose you find a wallet containing much money but also the card of the man who lost it – what would you do?"

The Jew answered, "You know, rabbi, that I have many children and am very poor. I would consider it as a gift from God. I would throw away the card and keep the money."

The rabbi said, "You are a thief. Sit there."

He then called a second Jew and put to him the same question. The reply was, "I would return the money immediately to its legitimate owner."

The rabbi said, "You are stupid. Sit near that other man."

He called a third Jew: "What would you do in such a case?"

The reply was, "I don't know. Everything depends upon the grace I will have from God at that moment."

The rabbi embraced him. "This is the right answer."

The devil is often with me in my cell. His first proposal was that I should decide to deny and be freed. When I refused, he appeared again in the guise of an angel of light: "Decide to die rather than yield to the Communists. Stick to this holy decision. May it happen as you decide." It was necessary to refuse this second subtle injunction too. Jesus had said in Gethsemane, "Not my will, but thine be done."

In the eighth degree of one of these occult initiations, you have to accept as a rule of life the sentences, "Believe nothing and dare everything," or its variation, "Nothing is true; everything is permitted."

When Marx was asked what maxim he preferred, he replied, "Doubt everything." I know it is not easy to believe something. Every religious, political or moral attitude has arguments for and against. I have spent long hours over the books of Zen, the Upanishads, Buddha, Zoroaster, the Talmud, the Kabala, the Koran, as well as atheist philosophers. There are so many interesting thoughts and persuasive proofs scattered throughout all of them. The sinner must choose with a limited, biased, unreliable mind that is only partially informed. But if a lost sinner has perforce a mind which cannot think rightly, he also cannot then believe that we are all lost sinners who cannot choose as we should.

If everything is only relatively true, the assertion about relativity is also only relatively true. There must be in relativity somewhere a kernel of the absolute. Life obliges you to dare, though what you do can produce enormous harm or good to someone else. I know a man who had taken in an orphan and given him a warm home. When this orphan grew up and married, he adopted another orphan child who was happy in new surroundings. So it is also with evil deeds. They reproduce endlessly.

In order to dare, I must have a standard of what is right and true.

Many religions offer ways of life. Jesus is not one of the ways. He says, "I am *the* way." The definite article is one of mankind's greatest devices. I am sorry for nations like China and Denmark that lack it.

Well, devil, you ask me to believe nothing. So I will turn this weapon against you and I will not believe that nothing should be believed. You say, "Nothing is true."

So the assertion that "nothing is true" is not true. You wish me to believe that "everything is permitted". All right, I will believe that it is also permitted *not* to believe that all things are permitted.

There were plenty of reasonable arguments for Romeo not to give his life for Juliet. Verona had many beautiful girls. He himself had been enamoured first of Rosaline. But a lover does not make his love the subject of arguments and counter-arguments. I hate your logic, devil. I love Jesus. I love His will. Let it be accomplished in my life. I love His laws and am always sorry whenever I break them because of my human weakness.

With me you have lost. The discussion with you has become boring. Goodbye. I prefer to go to sleep.

# NON-PERSON

DEAR BRETHREN AND SISTERS

On the first day of my arrest I had been told, "You are no more Richard Wurmbrand, but Vasile Georgescu. You are never allowed to mention to anyone your former name." I had been kidnapped from the street, and the simple fact that I still exist somewhere is a state secret. A warden might disclose it if he knew the name.

Today I protested against the mistreatment, saying, "Even if I don't belong to you, I am still a person, a man, and have the right to be respected."

They answered in a laugh: "What conceit! You are no longer a person. You simply are not. One thing exists: the proletarian state. Men belong to it. They are each a little wheel or a screw in its complex machinery. Whoever does not support the state simply is not. We don't even shoot him. There is nobody to shoot. We allow nothingness to rot away in a cell."

"I am not." "I am a nothing." Some philosophers say that the nothing exists somehow. If it does not exist, whose existence are we denying?

I remember the famous resumé of Buddha's doctrine from Vissudhimagga:

There exists only the suffering, not the sufferer.
There exists action, not its author.
The nirvana exists, but not the one who pursues it.

There is the way, but not the traveller.

I have had the shock of being told that I am a non-person. Now the non-person, no longer able even to wish to be a person, resigns itself to its new phase of existence. There is no more a man of sorrows in the cell; only the old, old sorrow is here, impersonal. My cell is old. Many generations of prisoners have experienced its sorrow before me, and many more will consider it their own after me. But suffering grants no one a monopoly. It wishes to be shared by everyone. Who has escaped its embrace?

Murder has existed since the time of Cain, but most murderers are unchronicled. Adultery has thrived down through the ages, but the Gospel does not even give the name of the woman caught in the act. What difference does her identity make? Lying affected the human situation in Paradise, before the Fall. Whoever utters a lie only adds his poison to the well.

Heaven also exists. If you pursue it, you do not have it. There should be no "you" and no "I". If these disappear, the pursuit ceases and heaven is within. It has always been there. The barrier has been "you" and the condition put by the "you", that your highest desires must be fulfilled. Heaven is the fulfilling of One's desires, the unique God. It might be His desire – it might be my heaven – that I lead the most annoying life in a solitary cell.

A heaven in which I do not rejoice? The Bible has told me to deny myself. I have neglected to do so. Now the Communists tell me that I have become a non-person. So who is the "I" that has the claim of rejoicing in heaven? Heaven is a place without distinction between the subject that enjoys, the object enjoyed, and the sentiment of joy. It simply exists. You are seated in "heavenly places" without striving for something beyond. For the first time a place where you really sit without any remorse for not doing something, without any need to move or fill your time with something else. It is rest, perfect rest.

When I was declared a non-person this morning, I told the captain, "Christ will be the victor through the patience that He gave us. A man with patience can do everything."

He laughed, "Can patience help you carry water in a sieve?"

I was disconcerted for a fraction of a second. Then I answered quietly, "For a certainty, if only you wait patiently for the water to freeze."

There is hope that they will make even living water freeze. It is terribly cold in the cell, though outside it must be the beginning of spring already. How I would like to be in the country and pick flowers, wild ones, hawthorns and violets and forget-me-nots. It is written, "Every one that loves is born of God" (1 John 4:7). But does anyone love if he does not include flowers in his love? Is it enough to love men?

I remember reading about an American black revolutionary, John Brown, who fought against slavery. His whole mature life was spent on riots. When he was led to the gallows in a cart, he said to the soldiers surrounding him, "How beautiful is this land." He had had no eyes for trees and flowers before. If I were free now, I would leave men alone and walk among foxgloves and daisies and dedicate myself to the good deed of loving flowers.

Flowers exist for us en masse. We don't attribute personality to them. Except for the florist when he sells them, we don't even give them a number. They don't worry about being non-persons. But they are loved by

Jesus. He compares Himself to them: "I am the rose of Sharon, and the lily of the valleys" (Song of Solomon 2:1).

If you wish to pluck them, they don't flee. If you trample them under your feet, they reward you by giving you their perfume. Jesus teaches us to learn from flowers. If I had been like one of them, I would not have cared about being appreciated.

I remember Feinstein, the man who played a big role in bringing me to Christ and who died a martyr's death under the Nazis. I asked him once, "What is the pride of life mentioned in 1 John 2:16?"

He replied, "Stop asking silly questions, you idiot."

I shouted, "How do you dare to speak to me like that?"

His answer: "Now you know what is the pride of life."

I believe that it is still a remnant of the pride of life that made me resent so vividly the words which I was told today – that I am a non-person.

I will accept my new status. Amen.

# DOES GOD AVENGE HIMSELF?

DEAR BRETHREN AND SISTERS

We Christians speak to our torturers about love. They speak only about hatred and revenge.

You can never understand any Communist if you don't see his wickedness as the result of intense suffering. No one becomes a trouble-maker unless he is greatly troubled himself. He takes revenge ultimately against being. He is without the desire for life itself. An absurd existence has been imposed upon him. He believes that a man is nothing more nor less than a random agglomeration of molecules. Among these molecules are those that constitute nerves, which sometimes produce feelings of joy (always transitory) and at other times transmit pain.

Communists cannot account for the fact that they have to endure suffering nor that eventually they will be eaten by worms. Therefore, they must make haste to enjoy life, power, and material advantages. In opposition to their presumed felicity are other agglomerations of molecules called class-enemies, which must be destroyed. Marx's favourite verse was, "There is no greater joy than to bite your enemy."

Our torturers see us as obstacles to their squeezing out of a senseless life the maximum of pleasant moments. Their conscience is not bothered by the fact that they beat human beings. When we ask why, they answer:

"Did you have any remorse when you hammered a nail into the wall or when you cut wood? We all handle matter at pleasure. Man too is only matter. You can't make an omelette without breaking eggshells. You can't cut wood without producing chips. You cannot make revolution without handling the class-enemy roughly. We know no forgiveness. We take revenge on our enemies."

Revenge sometimes arises from great depths. Marx once wrote to Engels, "If Titus had not destroyed my fatherland 1800 years ago, I would not be an enemy of all fatherlands."

When I am left alone in my cell, Bible verses come to my mind, but now they are different. A voice whispers, "Don't mind your sufferings. They don't pass unnoticed. The Lord will take revenge."

Again revenge? I cannot suffer the word any more. Should You, the Good, stoop to the same level as the Communists? Should heaven be reduced to the state of mind of a Communist torturer? I cannot believe these words about revenge, even if a St. Paul states them.

Should You, like Hitler, have burning ovens with unquenchable flames – no, even worse than Hitler, because his flames consumed the victims in a moment, whereas yours burn but never consume? Forgive us, but those in hell cannot accept the justice of hell. It is acceptable only to the man who sits in church after a good breakfast.

It might be that hell causes joy among saints. Saints are men, and nothing evil in men surprises me any more. But You are goodness personified. You can know happiness only through loving everybody, providing salvation, understanding, forgiving. If there is a hell, surely You must have the desire to quench its fire.

There certainly is a hell. You discharged in Yourself

the lightning of wrath when, torn by grief, You bruised Your Son and burdened Him with all the evil ever committed.

Yes, vengeance is Yours. As the sea absorbs the mighty rivers, You absorbed our rivers of wickedness and expiated them Yourself. This revenge is terrible. Because the death of Jesus on the cross burns the elect. This is the burning bush which is never consumed. It finishes with sin.

We know You to be love. You are our Father; Your Son, our Brother. Those who were once cold now burn with an eternal fire. It is the fire of love which has lit them.

I would believe You to be a God of love even if it were not reality. You are as I will You to be, not as You are. Love covers sin, and if I knew that You were vengeful, I would hide this fact from men. But no, You are forgiveness.

How torn I am. I began by not believing what St. Paul writes. Now I don't believe what I preach. The Word of God cannot be contradicted. It speaks clearly about an eternal hell. What kind of heaven would it be with Hitler and Stalin in it, with all the robbers and seducers and liars who have remained unregenerate to the end? One serpent in the Garden – and mankind lost Paradise. How will heaven remain unsullied if men who are not born again invade its precincts?

The idea that men will be tormented forever is unbearable to me. But are the unrepentant sinners men? I have no remorse about killing tuberculosis microbes. I am happy that DDT wiped out vermin. A sinner, yes, even a criminal, has something human in him until the last moment of his death, after which he ceases to be human. His wickedness alone remains, self-conscious utter wickedness. We cannot imagine this, but the whole of reality is unimaginable. The atom is unimaginable. It is not in vain that God told us not to make ourselves images of things. God considered it proper that strange beings like this, for whom we will feel no affinity at all, should burn eternally.

And then, hell might not be as unbearable and terrible as we think. St. Paul said, "I could wish that myself were accursed from Christ for my brethren" (Rom. 9:3). This means that perfect saints can renounce heaven. In Buddhism, the perfect, the Boddhisatvas, refuse to enter Nirvana before drawing all men with them. Likewise saints who have experienced the rich love of God can bear hell. Saints around me bear the hell of Communist prison. Some of them bear it joyfully. I think that hell accepted with love ceases to be hell. St. Paul would not have feared to be accursed. He would have taken the doom with passionate love in order that it might profit others.

Christ Himself was damned and abandoned more than all the saints. So for the children of God there can be a heaven in hell. The terribleness of hell is only for the others. God gives everyone His fit place - water for fish, air for birds, jail for criminals. Hell is the fit place for unrepentant sinners.

We will never be able to accept it until all our fixed ideas about God and eternal things are broken up and discarded, even the notion that God is good, a notion that is false if God's goodness is separated from His many other attributes that qualify it, as, for example, His righteousness. "The kingdom of Heaven is like unto treasure hid in a field" (Matt. 13:44). "Your life is hid with Christ in God" (Col. 3:3).

There exists the unintelligible in Godhead. We must believe His Word even if it contradicts our notions of what we consider right for God to do. The virgin Mary

143

was told that her Son would be given the throne of His father David, and this she doubtless accepted at face value. Instead, He was mocked and He descended into hell. St. Augustine, contrary to the prayerful expectations of his mother Monica, descended deeper and deeper into sin before God not only answered her prayers for his conversion but made of him a great Christian teacher.

We cannot understand God's ways. We must believe in His revelation. I cannot understand hell. I would send nobody to an eternal hell. But happily God is not like me. If He were, He would not give me paradise. I have to sacrifice the intellect. I believe in eternal hell. I believe that God avenges Himself. "To me belongeth vengeance, and recompence", "Vengeance is mine; I will repay, saith the Lord" (Deut. 32:35; Rom. 12:19).

May God keep me from being the object of His revenge. Amen.

# MY UNFINISHED REQUIEM

DEAR BRETHREN AND SISTERS
  As usual, I start my night-vigil by singing softly
Mozart's *Requiem*:

> On that great, that awful day,
> This vain world shall pass away.
> Thus the sibyl sang of old,
> Thus has holy David told;
> There shall be a deadly fear
> When the Avenger shall appear,
> And unveiled before His eye,
> All the works of men shall lie.
> Hark! to the great trumpet's tones
> Pealing o'er the place of bones;
> Hark! it waketh from their bed
> All the nations of the dead,
> In a countless throng to meet
> At the eternal judgment seat.
> Nature sickens with dismay;
> Death may not retain his prey,
> And before the Maker stand
> All the creatures of His hand.
> The great book shall be unfurled,
> Whereby God shall judge the world:
> What was distant, shall be near,
> What was hidden, shall be clear.

## Alone With God

To what shelter shall I fly?
To what guardian shall I cry?
O, in that destroying hour,
Source of goodness, source of power,
Show Thou, of Thine own free grace,
Help unto a helpless race!
Tho' I plead not at Thy throne,
Aught that I for Thee have done,
Do not Thou unmindful be,
Of what Thou hast borne for me;
Of the wandering, of the scorn,
Of the scourge, and of the thorn.
Jesus, hast Thou borne the pain,
And hath all been borne in vain?
Shall Thy vengeance smite the head
For whose ransom Thou hast bled?
Thou, whose dying blessing gave
Glory to a guilty slave:
Thou, who from the crew unclean
Did'st release the Magdalene:
Shall not mercy, vast and free,
Evermore be found in Thee?
Father, turn on me Thine eyes,
See my blushes, hear my cries;
Faint tho' be the cries I make,
Save me, for Thy mercy's sake,
From the worm, and from the fire,
From the torments of Thine ire.
Fold me with the sheep that stand
Pure and safe at Thy right hand.
Hear Thy guilty child implore Thee,
Rolling in the dust before Thee.
O, the horrors of that day!
When this frame of sinful clay,
Starting from its burial place,

## My Unfinished Requiem

Must behold Thee face to face.
Hear and pity, hear and aid,
Spare the creatures Thou hast made.
Mercy, mercy, save, forgive:
O who shall look on Thee and live?
(English translation by Thomas Macaulay; in
*Seed Thoughts for Public Speakers*)

Though the *Requiem* had been commissioned, Mozart composed it for himself. During that time he was already very sick, as I am now.

I could say about myself what Mozart wrote when he created this music:

In my soul I have chaos. I can gather my thoughts only with difficulty. I see unceasingly the face of one unknown. He insists. He asks me to work. I continue to do so, because to compose music wearies me less than inactivity. I feel my hour has come. I must die. The end comes before I can show fully my talent. How beautiful is life! But I must finish my burial-song. I would not do right to leave it unfinished.

I also try to put into these sermons declaimed in a solitary cell my deepest, perhaps my ultimate, dying thoughts. Such thoughts I could not propound from the pulpit, because there one has to preach according to dogma and the taste of the audience, with the goal of attracting new souls into the church. Here I have absolutely no aim, no purpose. I preach only because it is in my character to do so, as it is in the nature of nightingales to sing.

Mozart did not finish his *Requiem*. I might die or, perhaps, be freed before finishing my task. The worst, I think, would be to regain freedom and resume preaching conventional sermons.

While lying on his deathbed, Mozart could ask his friend Sussmeyer to finish the *Requiem*. Sussmeyer was able to transcribe some of the tunes from the lips of the dying man. I am absolutely alone. I can convey to no one my thoughts. Jesus left this world without having delivered all His message. On the last evening spent with His closest friends, He said, "I have yet many things to say unto you, but ye cannot bear them now" (John 16:12).

While Mozart lay on his deathbed, he was afforded the consolation of having his unfinished *Requiem* completed by a couple of friends. I will probably never see anyone feeding on these my sermons. At his burial, the burial of a beggar, there was no organ music, no ceremony, no money even for a grave-marker, much less a tombstone. Unmarked, too, are the graves of prisoners.

There were rumours that Mozart had been poisoned. He himself suspected it. But in his *Requiem* there is no complaint. He thinks only about his own sins and the judgment that lies before him, to which he will answer. There are probably drugs in my food. I become weaker and weaker. But I will not think badly about my enemies. I will not think about them at all.

In the Philippines, people have been found still living in the stone age. It pleases me that they have no words for "enemy" and "war". They can't be taught to love their foes. They have none.

I will sing my requiem while lying on planks that might later be used for my coffin. My soul is far from my body. There is no doubt that the soul lives after death. I am the proof. My body has long since been dead. But I live.

Rather, it is not the "I" which lives, but a huge regret

for what I have been, with tears running from the eyes of a corpse. The Orthodox believe in some weeping icons of the Virgin. Others say that it is a priestly trick, with some tubes and a pump hidden behind the icon. But why should wood not weep when a corpse can?

Oscar Wilde had been in my state when he composed "The Ballad of Reading Gaol". I begin my requiem with music to the words of his first stanzas:

> Yet each man kills the thing he loves,
>     By each let this be heard,
> Some do it with a bitter look,
>     Some with a flattering word,
> The coward does it with a kiss,
>     The brave man with a sword!
>
> Some kill their love when they are young,
>     And some when they are old;
> Some strangle with the hands of Lust,
>     Some with the hands of Gold:
> The kindest use a knife, because
>     The dead so soon grow cold.
>
> Some love too little, some too long,
>     Some sell, and others buy;
> Some do the deed with many tears,
>     And some without a sigh:
> For each man kills the thing he loves,
>     Yet each man does not die.

I also love men. Since my youth I have loved on sight every man I ever met. But I loved with a deadly love, because all my beloved have died or at least suffered much because of me. I don't believe like Wilde that each man kills the thing he loves. But I have. My one joy now is to have the world isolated from me so that I can no longer harm anyone.

Am I now being punished by God for my sins? The answer to this question is contained in the Persian poem *Rabbia*, which I remember. Set to melody, it is the second theme of my requiem:

> Rabbia, sick and abed,
> Was visited by two saints:
> The pious Malik, the sage Hassan,
> Men venerated in Islam.
> One said, "You'll be able to bear
> The chastising God sends you
> If your prayer is pure." The other,
> Profounder, gave his opinion:
> "If it is accepted with love,
> You rejoice about the punishment."
> Rabbia discerned traces
> Of egotism in these maxims.
> "Good men," he replied,
> "When one sees the face of the Master
> In his prayer, he cannot
> Remember that he is punished."

Before the Lord I simply am what I am, without any why. Why was I born? Why was I born a sinner? Why did I suffer? Why did I produce suffering? Why do I die? Why have I the gift of composing a kind of requiem? What is the good of composing it while alone in a prison cell? My God, my God, why have You forsaken me? Whys are futile. There is never any answer.

I am not being punished. Neither am I a martyr. How can I know what counts more in the depths of my heart: fanatical devotion to the anti-Communist fight or love for Christ? And even if it were martyrdom, what would be its value if it is based on a love which kills – a sentiment unworthy the name of love? Calvin said that where this love is wanting, "the beauty of all virtue is mere tinsel, is empty sound, is not worth a straw, nay more, is offensive and disgusting." Martyrdom minus genuine love equals zero.

Punished criminal or martyr, my last song is about Jesus, except that in my requiem, unlike Mozart's, it is not a song of fear and trembling. It bespeaks confidence.

When asked to descend from the cross, Jesus did not move. Were nails more powerful than the hands of the Son of God? On several occasions when large crowds had sought to molest Him, He escaped. Yet alone, armed only with a whip, He had challenged the unholy practices of a courtyard full of merchants guarded by the temple police – and escaped unharmed. He said "I AM" in Gethsemane, and a company of soldiers fell to the ground.

No, it was not nails that kept Jesus on the cross, but His love for me. For me, a non-person. Jesus loves the Father and He loves me. "The Son of man is come to seek and to save that which was lost" (Luke 19:10). I prefer to be a lost sinner rather than a martyr, because it is lost sinners He came to save.

Listen to me. The one who calls is one who always killed those he loved, who made people shed tears and blood. You who give life to those who hate, save one who spreads death even upon the most beloved.

The power fails me to continue. I am hungry. I have a high fever. My mind goes blank. I cannot put in song Jesus' answer to my cry.

This will remain my unfinished requiem. Amen.

# EPILOGUE

These sermons have had one subject: God as reflected in
deep human suffering. Only God is the subject.
Narrowness of scope is the only way to ensure critical
focus in spiritual matters. The waters of human nature
run deep, but if they are spread over a wide area, of
necessity they become shallow. With too many subjects
to cover, a man disperses his energy and dissipates his
vitality.

It is better to do one little thing well than to do many
things badly. Therefore I have striven to do just one
thing, to say what God is like when observed from the
perspective of an isolated subterranean prison cell and
to focus on the rapport that existed between Him and a
creature abandoned to hunger and torture. I hope this
might be helpful to others who pass through pain and
sorrow and who encounter problems of another kind.

I meant also to awaken in believers and men of good
will outside Christian circles the desire to do something
for the many thousands who are still imprisoned for
their faith.

What could *you* do?

I once told Isaac Feinstein, who died a martyr's death
under the Nazis, "The words of the Lord that He is 'the
way' are not of much practical use. After reading them,
you still don't know the next step. Now tell me plainly,
what is 'the way'?" He answered, "Go away." The

words would have sounded insulting were it not for his unequalled smile. His face and gestures gave to his words the meaning, "There is no answer to the question 'What is the way?' Jesus intended us to walk in it, not to inquire into it."

Before Jesus said "I am the way," He had already said, "The way ye know" (John 14:4). He is not a way we have to learn but one with which we are acquainted. We might not know the whole of it. We surely know the next few steps.

I will not tell you what to do in order to show compassion to those who today pass through the outer and inner tempests I have known. The simple fact that you have the desire to be helpful indicates that you need no guide. Your own compassionate nature will guide you.

Every step in this direction will also become a restraint not to act. From an eternal point of view, all activity, even holy activity, is counted among the vanities. How can someone do something without mixing into his purely idealistic endeavours some egotism, some calculation, some desire to impress? Busy yourself with good works, and you may suddenly stop walking in the way in order to sit like Mary at the feet of Jesus, choosing "that good part, which shall not be taken away" rather than the busy work of Martha. You then become a passionate lover of God, seeking to adore Him even if He allows you to pass through terrible circumstances, such as I have known.

The next step? You have stopped walking, and there will be no more steps. Adoring Him, you will realise in time that you have become more than a mere believer, because a believer is not satisfied with worship. A young man will not simply adore a girl lifelong. He will be satisfied with nothing less than possessing her, uniting with her. So you will pass from adoring God to being one in spirit with Christ and, through Him, with the Father. It will be God who suffers in you for His creation, but through Him you will be at last triumphant.

With this the aim of my book will have been achieved. God has kept these sermons in my memory in spite of brainwashing and doping with drugs. In jail I lost all my knowledge of music and mathematics. I forgot even the Bible. But I remembered these sermons, because God willed you to read them and be changed from glory to glory in the likeness of His Son. Praise be to Him!

The words "Praise the Lord" occur in the Bible 366 times, once for every day of the year, including leap year. The Lord had to be praised in cells infested with rats and vermin, in days when we were badly beaten. The Lord should be praised daily by you, too, amid the troubles through which you pass.

*Praised be the Lord!* When you say it, you will realise you knew the next step in "the way".

For current information on the
Persecuted Church contact:

# The Voice of the Martyrs, Inc.
PO Box 443
Bartlesville, OK 74005
(918) 337-8015

# FROM THE LIPS OF CHILDREN

*Richard Wurmbrand*

'The Bible is meant for children. Only the children of Israel came out of slavery in Egypt; the grown-ups stayed behind. Only the children of God enter heaven. It will be a country without any grown-ups.'

This observation by Richard Wurmbrand's grandson Alex is just one of the many delightful anecdotes and children's sayings in this attractively illustrated volume. Children's insights sharpen adults' minds and in collecting and commenting on them – many from behind the Iron Curtain – Pastor Wurmbrand challenges Christians to take seriously Jesus' teaching that his followers must become like children.

'A delightful book that can be picked up and read at any time . . . one that will not fail to bring joy . . . to us grown-ups.'

*Evangelism Today*

'Challenges us to think about our own faith.'

*Redemption*